SUBMARINE MEMORIES

OUR TIME IN 'BOATS'

SOME OF THE LESSER KNOWN FACTS FROM THE GATWICK SUBMARINE ARCHIVE

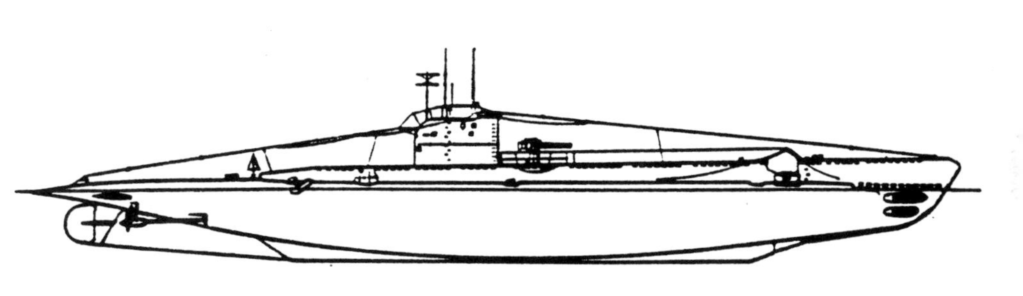

EDITED BY THE ARCHIVE COMMITTEE:
Keith Nethercoate-Bryant
Ron Hart BEM
Colin Hunt
Stan Murray

Foreword

Rear Admiral Ben Bryant CB. DSO★★. DSC

One of the most satisfying things for an 'old timer', is to see how the Submarine Old Comrades Association goes from strength to strength. I did my training class, then a simple affair, in 1927, when you still met people who had served in 'A' boats. The Officer's training class relied nearly entirely on two personalities; an engineer lieutenant who had come up the hard way, and a chief T.G.M.
We had to expect everything in a boat to be apt to break down, and the engineer seemed always to end his description of any piece of machinery by saying how it "Fell over for a pastime". The chief T.G.M. immensely versatile, dealt with the rest, except when we got in a C.P.O. Tel from outside to deal with the W.T.
The Submarine Service was then the Cinderella of the Royal Navy, looked on by some as not quite respectable. But that did not worry the submariners, who developed a tremendous 'Esprit de Corps', which has persisted to this day.
There is a hymn which starts 'Through all the changing scenes of life' and this rather describes how the spirit of the early submariners persists in the large, complicated, immensely powerful boats of today.

Ben Bryant

Introduction

This little booklet of undersea odds and ends has been produced by the Gatwick Submarine Archive under the auspices of the Gatwick Branch of the Submarine Old Comrades Association. The profits from its sale will contribute to the funding of the Archive, the 'Submarine Memorial Fund' and our branch adopted charity R.N.B.T. 'Pembroke House' Gillingham.

The Archive was founded in 1988 to record the Gatwick Branch members ephemera, anecdotes, photographs and their memories of the Submarine Service in war and peace. With the enthusiastic help from members of many other branches of S.O.C.A., we have progressed from what was purely a local exercise to an ongoing rescue campaign which now includes members of the International Submarine Association.

Many of the surviving wartime crew members are now in their sixties and beyond, once they have slipped their anchor there is no one to identify their 'oppos' who may feature in their personal photographs. Many of these photos were taken with cameras that were not officially permitted in wartime, therefore a great many have not yet been seen by anyone other than that submariner's family and friends.

Apart from research by crew members descendants tracing their ancestors and historians after Naval incidents no one can fully appreciate the use to which a collection of material such as ours will be put to in the future. These little windows into the past are moments of submarine history frozen in time. It is our duty to preserve as much as we can for future generations.

We are operating this Archive with the help and co-operation of the Submarine Museum at Gosport and are not in any way a rival organisation. We have had much help with our displays and exhibitions from that doyen of Submarine Historians, 'Gus' Britton and the present curator Margaret Bidmead. Our collection is open to all, most of our material is recorded onto slides as a permanent record which enables us to stage an 'Evening of Memories' each May. Anyone willing to loan us any of their treasured items can be safe in the knowledge that we have our own photographer, where possible photos, etc. are returned personally or sent through the post by registered or recorded delivery.

Keith Nethercoate-Bryant
Chairman Gatwick S. O. C. A.

Dedication

We would like to dedicate this book to the memory of Peter Darby and Ted Pratt, who have both crossed the bar.

Peter was a past chairman of the Gatwick S.O.C.A. and a submariner of over twenty years service who had supported the idea of an archive and helped bring it into being.

Ted was one of the founder members of the Gatwick branch of the, Submarine Old Comrades Association. He was a long serving submariner and was vice-chairman of the branch on several occasions.

Peter Darby

Ted Pratt

Acknowledgements

Our grateful thanks are due to the Submarine Museum at Gosport, Imperial War Museum, S.O.C.A. branches in Britain, Australia and New Zealand. The International Submarine Association, Horst Bredow of the U-Boat Archive. Walter Cloots, researcher (Belgium). Many SOCA and ISA members have given us much help but are too numerous to mention here. However major research and photographs have been given to us by Gus Britton (Former Assistant Director Submarine Museum), Margaret Bidmead (Curator Sub. Mus.), Charles Beattie, Bill Britton Snr., Paul Chapman DSO. OBE. DSC★(Torbay), Frank Dedman, Syd Denham DSM★ BEM, A. Dickison, Ken Dixon, Dick Duffield, Dickie Elliott, Tony Farrant, Peter Freeland, Keith Fuller (ISA), Frank Gapper, David Gilbertson, Ray Gritt, Nina & Douglas Hamilton, Peter House, Stan Jones, John Maber, John Patrick, Tom Perrin, Geo Pickup, Jack Pollard, Phil Prew, Lt. Com. Dick Raikes DSO, Jack Reeve, Doug Shepherd, Bill Sherrington, Dr. D. Sinclair, Eric Springford, Dr. Ken Wade DSM, Alec Wingrave.

John Capes MSS. Loaned by his daughter Julie and son Gregory.

Line Drawings from P. Akerman, The Encyclopedia of British Submarines 1901-1955 by kind permission of Maritime Books.

Contents

H. M. Submarine M2. 1
H. M. Submarine X1. 3
H. M. Submarine M1. 4
H. M. Submarine K26. 5
Submarine Safari And The Tank. 6
J. H. Capes. 17
Why He Was Called Crash. 42
H. M. Submarine Strongbow. 43
Notes From The Diary Of Lt. Com. Dick Raikes D.S.O. . 54
Springer, Scorcher And Sportsman. 59
U-1105 Black Panther. 60
My Early Submarine Memories - A. 'Tancy' Lee. . . 65
Wartime Poet Inspired By Campbeltown. . . . 67
The First Commission Of H.M.Submarine Sibyl. . . 68
A B.N.L.O. In Dutch And French Submarines. . . 75
The Egg In The Oyster. 80
Surrender Of U-2326 At Dundee. 84
His Majesty's Submarine Ambush. 88
His Majesty's Canadian U-Boat U-190. 92
U-1407 H.M.Submarine Meteorite. 95
H. M. Submarine Artemis. 96
H. M. Submarine Satyr. 107
A True Yarn. 110
H. M. Submarine Unruly. 111
H. M. Submarine Grampus In The Arctic. . . . 112
H. M. Submarine Aeneas. 113
H. M. Submarine Turpin. 116
Hauling In The Hoses. 117
Photographs From A Naval Airship 118
H. M. Submarine Affray. 120
H. M. Submarine Token. 121
H. M. Submarine Tireless. 122
U-792 And U-793 At Kiel. 123
H. M. Submarine Shakespeare. 124

H. M. Submarine M. 2. (see Front Cover)

M. 2. is shown catapulting off the Parnell Peto seaplane some time after 1925. Originally fitted with a 12" gun was converted to carry one seaplane for scouting purposes. She was also armed with torpedoes and smaller caliber guns. She was lost in 1932 during exercises when the boat was flooded through the hanger, there were no survivors and sixty including RAF airmen perished.
M. 1. fitted with a 12" gun and developed out of the earlier steam K class hull was lost due to collision in 1925 with a loss of sixty-nine lives, there were no survivors.
M. 3. was converted to carry up to 100 mines around 1927. She was launched in 1916 and was converted to a minelaying submarine in 1927. Her mines weighed something over 1000 lbs each. Many Londoners (of mature years) may remember her supplying electricity to the London Docks in 1926 during the National Strike in May of that year. She was broken up in 1932.
These were huge submarines in the inter war years displacing over 2000 tons; others later overshadowed them; X. 1. of 3000 tons plus, mounting four 5.2" guns. Surcouf the French submarine with two 8" guns and carrying a seaplane in a hanger aft of the conning tower. The Japanese built three 5000 ton submarines designed to carry three aeroplanes. All were giants of their time but are dwarfed by todays true submarines. Consider the Russian 'Typhoon' class at 27,000 - 30,000 tons, the same displacement as WWII battleships.

IN MEMORIAM.

✝

H.M. SUBMARINE M.2

SUNK OFF PORTLAND

TUESDAY, JANUARY 26th, 1932.

Once again comes the sad story of disaster to a British Submarine
Sucked down by seething waters, which their lives had come between ;
She was out for a day's manœuvres,
Accompanied by more Submarines,
But, the trip, as we now know was to be her last.

A search was quickly started by Tenders close at hand,
And a message despatched for help, to their comrades on the land,
The salvage plant, and tugs were ordered to the scene,
To help and assist, if possible, those men in the Submarine

A few more hearts are breaking a few more tears are shed,
By mothers and wives in England, for their bread winners now dead ;
Drawn down to the hungry depths, so many fathoms deep,
They now lie in that Submarine M.2, sleeping their long last sleep.

They were only doing their duty, but their hearts were blithe and gay,
Little dreaming of the awful fate awaiting them that day ;
Destroyers and Sweepers are keeping vigil o'er the brave.
And have flown their flags at half-mast, to salute a Sailor's Grave.

In the midst of life, we are in death, that's what our prayer books say,
And in the British Navy, it is proven every day,
For men that go to sea in ships, their Country to uphold,
Carry their lives at their finger tips, but do as they are told.

But now let us turn to the dear ones, the dead have left behind,
It is our duty to assist them, which we must bear in mind,
So turn your thoughts towards them ; now devoid of means ;
And help the mothers, wives and children of men drowned in Submarines.

G. WATSON,
Leading Stoker.

The Giant Experimental Boat HMS/M X1

HMS/M M.1 - Constantinople

HMS/M M.1 - Shotley

The Steam Submarine HMS/M K.26

Submarine Safari And The Tank.
North Africa

The submarine contribution to the North African landings, apart from the cloak-and-dagger operations landing agents beforehand, was to cover the invasion in case the Italian Fleet ventured out. I had by now spent a good deal of time in patrolling on Thin Red Lines, Iron Rings, Dunkirk, Malta Convoys and so forth to intercept German and Italian Fleets which did not materialise and I viewed the prospect without enthusiasm. We were, with a number of other boats of the Malta Flotilla, strung out between Sicily and Sardinia and, as usual, nothing came our way. However P.46, later to be called Unruffled, a name which aptly described her C.O. (Lieutenant Stevens, DSO, DSC), got in an attack on a new cruiser of the 'Regolo' class. She winged it and we looked on enviously at the clouds of smoke over the horizon and listened, not so enviously, to the depth-charging which was the inevitable sequel.

It was a Sunday and that evening as we were having our Sunday Service in the control room, Paris, the Petty Officer Telegraphist, brought me a signal from Shrimp Simpson. It read: Damaged enemy cruiser N. E. of Cape St. Vito in tow with eight destroyers, six E-boats and aircraft in company. P.44 close immediately. P.211 (Safari) proceed to C. Gallo to intercept.

In his covering report on these operations, Shrimp said: In two years of operating the Tenth Flotilla I must remark that I have never felt more conscious of my arm-chair directorate than in making this signal to P.211 and P.44. I had the advantage of knowing that both Lieutenant Barlow (P.44) and Commander Bryant had experience and a sense of humour. It was a tremendous screen for a single ship and there must have been nearly record odds against the submarine.

It was nice to be released from the boring patrol line, but the prospect of being mixed up with this party on the surface at night in inshore waters was a bit sobering. I reckoned that our interception could wait a few minutes whilst we finished the Service and maybe a little more fervour went into the prayers.

I dare say that many Services have been held in stranger places, but no one would have missed our little Sunday Service in the control room;

the officer of the watch scanning around on the periscope, the planesman controlling the depth, the helmsman his wheel, an occasional trimming order. One particular prayer - it is not to be found in any prayer book and I forgot where I found it, though I believe it is called the Knight's Prayer - was particularly pugnacious and we looked upon it as our own. Everyone who could, crowded into the control room, oil-stained and un-shaven, and just outside the Roman Catholics, the only denomination who could not join in, would collect for the sermon. I regret to say that it was a bit secular; it covered what we had done the previous week, together with any general information. On this occasion, I read out Shrimp's signal, which was greeted with the usual imperturbability. We then surfaced and worked up to full power as we made for Cape Gallo near Palermo.

Sunday was reckoned a lucky day in Safari, we had once sighted a ship during the Service and had to break off to sink it, but on this occasion, we never found the cruiser. It was before the days of radar as far as Safari and the Italians were concerned. Night work was just a matter of seeing without being seen and, as we closed Cape Gallo two hours later, we had to cut down our speed or the wake and bow wave would have given us away.

It was a dark night, it was hard to see under the cliffs, and we were coming in from seaward. We were very close to the first destroyer when we saw her and had to dive in a hurry. From 19.45 to 01.00 we were in amongst the screen, occasionally diving for a few minutes when one got too close, most of the time on the surface. First we had to work through them to get under the cliffs ourselves, thus being able to see better to seaward, hoping to find the cruiser on the way, but we were continually thwarted. The screen was weaving about, fourteen of them covered a good deal of sea, and we had constantly to take evasive action. For over five hours there were seldom less than two destroyers in sight. We did finally get through under the cliffs but we never found the cruiser.

It must be remembered that visibility on such a night even with excellent binoculars was not much over a mile under the cliffs; we were frequently within 600 yards of destroyers, our speed reduced to avoid wake; our target could have been anywhere within an area of about seventy-five square miles and every time we were forced to dive, we lost distance. Surfacing again in such circumstances is not without interest; you could not range, you just judged from the propeller noises how far

HMS/M Safari Algiers - April 1943

Goodbye Malta. Ben Bryant - January 1943

Safari's Crew Algiers - 1943

Supply Ship with petrol & ammunition for Rommel's desert army, Gulf of Gabes Tunisia. Results of Safari's gun action - 13th December 1942.

away your nearest opponent might be - and part of enemy hydrophone technique was to stop and listen; if they did that you could easily come alongside one unless you keep tabs on everyone in the vicinity.

The Asdic operators had a tremendous responsibility.

By 01.00 it became evident that the cruiser had made her escape to Palermo and even though her screen failed to see or detect us, they had served their purpose. We had had a very strenuous five hours. Had we allowed one of the destroyers to see us I should probably not be writing the story. Our eyes were nearly hanging out; failure is so often harder work than success.

It was a great relief not to be sent back on the patrol line; all our submarines were concentrated in the Central Mediterranean. The initial landings had been achieved but the reactions of the French in North Africa were unknown; we were dispatched to Susa, east of Tunis, to report the situation.

We threaded our way through the minefields of the Sicilian Channel, an area where the turtles which so closely resembled mines awash would collect and cause much unnecessary anxiety, and then made off on the surface for Susa. The French Tricolour was still flying over the citadel as we closed submerged and there was no sign of activity; it was rather hard to know how to collect information.

An Italian auxiliary brigatine of some four hundred tons, carrying stores to Rommel' s army, blundered into our deliberations; and, in due course, down she went. We picked up a couple of chaps swimming in the water and went alongside a boat to deposit them; we demanded that "El Capitano" should come on board. The whole boat-load immediately leapt aboard and eventually No. 1 picked out the Captain; the enthusiasm of the rest to join us necessitated their being pushed back into the water.

We had given them time to take to their boats before opening fire, an old fashioned courtesy seldom possible in these days of air patrols, and presumably they thought us nice chaps. In any case, the Sicilians had no enthusiasm for the war, the Germans by this time had made themselves far more unpopular than anyone else, and the little boat-load gave us an enthusiastic send off as we left them to row into Susa. I thought the Captain might give us some useful information. As he went down through the conning-tower hatch, Devlin, the navigator, noted some papers in his breast pocket and fished them out - they included the

Italian recognition signals for the next week and also route orders and some very useful navigational data which we signalled back to Malta.
Our next orders were to move east with all despatch; a German patrol ship had been reported making for the battle front. The Eighth Army had won Alamein, but had not yet reached Benghazi. Our boats had kept Rommel woefully short of petrol - I believe that shortage of petrol had a significant effect upon the battles - and the Germans were seizing on our pre-occupation with the Algiers landing to run in a ship.
Normally, one would not have gone on the surface by day in these waters; but reckoning that everyone was fairly well occupied elsewhere, a home-made Italian Ensign fluttering bravely and armed with recognition signals, Chiefy Harris and his engine room were soon coaxing every possible revolution out of the diesels as we made off on the surface to the eastward.
On the second morning as dawn broke we were closing Ras Ali in the southeast corner of the Gulf of Sidra when we spotted a ship making away northward towards Benghazi. This was doubtless our quarry.
Our approach must have been reported by the numerous transport aircraft, the position checked against enemy submarine dispositions, and the ensign established as bogus. We set off in chase. We would have to work round ahead of her to get in an attack, keeping below her horizon, then dive and wait. It was an exciting chase; we were near the battle area, transport planes and landing craft were frequent and it could not be long before a Ju.88 was dispatched to deal with us.
We had to be satisfied with just keeping her mast heads above the horizon; occasionally her crow' s nest would come clear, which meant that anyone in it could also see our bridge. She was pursuing a most erratic course and judging the alterations with just those two masts to go was not easy. Every minute counted; at one time it would seem that we were doing nicely, then an alteration of course would throw it all out.
I learned later that the operations room at Malta was following all this from the German signals; the ship was of vital importance; loaded with cased petrol she not unnaturally had the wind up and was calling plaintively for help, but the Italian Fleet was elsewhere. By now she must have been receiving reports of our presence; we could not afford to waste time by diving for the innumerable transport aircraft.
At last, towards noon, just as we were working into our position to dive ahead, she turned right round.

Safari's Jolly Roger recording ships torpedoed, sunk by gun action, cloak & dagger operations, the lighthouse denotes the submarine was used as a homing beacon for the invasion of Sicily.

Back in the U.K.

AB. McDonald, Tel. A. Dickinson, AB. Craig, AB. Tallamy (Gunlayer), P.O. TGM. McIntyre.

Safari returns after 18 months Med. Commission to HMS Forth
19th September 1943

For nearly two days the engine room had been doing virtually a full power trial and now all was set at nought. The A/S air patrols arrived; we could not continue the chase and were forced to dive. I reckoned she would make back for Ras Ali, where there was a small stone landing pier on the desert beach.

The North African desert shore is not a nice place to close at night; it is low and shallow for a long way to seaward so the soundings give you little help.

There was a moon that night, and choosing the time when it would be to the southward, and therefore helping us, we closed the coast. The water became too shallow to dive, but hidden against the sand dunes we found her. She was lying at rather an awkward angle and we had to creep rather close inshore to get a shot; she appeared to be surrounded by E-boats, small dark shapes in the moonlight, not nice things to encounter in water too shallow to dive. The sights came on, the torpedo fled the tube leaving a silver ribbon on the dappled waters.

We had to wait and see if it ran true before retiring, but ran true it did. Suddenly it was broad daylight. The ship went up in a sheet of flame, and here we were, right into the enemy shore in shallow water infested by E-boats, plain for all to see. The tail rattled as the helm went hard over when I called for emergency full speed. The boat turned sluggishly in the shallow water and we felt terribly naked in that brilliant illumination.

The anti-climax was that no-one took the slightest notice of us, there was nothing to worry about; the "E-boats" were only landing craft. But for those who like fireworks, it was certainly a rousing sight.

I thought of our prisoner, who had apparently become very depressed. He was living in the E.R.A.'s mess and spent all his days sleeping under the table; I thought a little fresh air and a pyrotechnic display, especially as he had no love for the Germans, might cheer him up. I asked him to come up as we headed for deeper water, but his depression was too deep to be relieved. It turned out that his trouble was constipation; there was a language difficulty but things can be conveyed by signs. This was well within my medical repertoire. I prescribed a "Number nine" - popularly supposed, like faith, to move mountains. The depression continued. I prescribed two number nines. Then three. No relief; something that could not be cleared by three number nines was beyond my medical competence; the possible effect of building up number nines further was alarming. He must wait for proper medical attention when we got in; meanwhile he continued sleeping under the table.

When we got in he was sent up to the interrogation centre and a couple of days later I met an officer who worked there and enquired after my friend. He said at first they could get no information out of him, he could only ask for a purge.

The doctors purged him and once more he came up for interrogation; as usual, they first asked him how he had been treated.

He said: "The Captain he was very kind to me; he treated me as one gentleman to another gentleman; he gave me these," and putting his hand in his waistcoat pocket produced the six number nines; he had kept them as curios.

Possibly he thought they were not meant to be eaten, except by horses.

The landing craft were to cause some amusement in the next couple of days. The bigger ones were called Siebel ferries and they had a formidable armament. Some carried a German 88mm and all seemed to carry Bofors, quite a lethal weapon, even though smaller than our 3-inch (75mm) and a quarter of a century later in design than that ancient model. Like us, the landing craft presented a low silhouette and were hard to hit; we had some stimulating exchanges of cannonry with them. Their automatic armament, fitted for use against attack by aircraft, used fixed fuses, which exploded at about 2,500 to 3,000 yards. One had to keep outside that. Between us and the landing craft would be a scintillating wall of balls of cotton wool, with the water boiling as the fuses exploded short. There was still some interest in their fire, as not all fuses exploded to order.

We were not very clever with them; they could absorb quite a lot of our 3 inch and we had difficulty in hitting them at all. We were also short of ammunition, normally on such a patrol every nook and cranny, even the passageways, would be strewn with ammunition. But we had started this patrol to attack the Italian Fleet; loose ammunition is a hazard when you are being thrown about by a depth-charge attack and we had taken little beyond the designed stowage which, although it obeyed the explosive regulations, was otherwise inadequate. However, we did set a couple on fire, but what with their guns and A/S aircraft always turning up at an awkward moment it was not very satisfactory. They were too shallow draft to torpedo normally, but we did have a satisfying crack at them at Ras Ali pier the morning after getting the petrol ship. She had

capsized and sunk; her hull still showed above water and from it came little spouts of flame all next day. The sea was strewn with 50-gallon drums, floating awash so that they were difficult to see and a danger to the periscope.
In that shallow water and against a bottom of silver sand, a submarine would normally show up clearly to aircraft, but there was a nice chop on the water and we managed to get in to 4,500 yards before it became too shallow. Ras Ali pier was packed with landing craft; we fired a torpedo set to very shallow to run over the shoals, it ran dead true to the pier and there followed a truly remarkable explosion; there must have been some ammunition lighters among them. When the explosion died down you could see lots of little black figures scurrying up the sand dunes. There had been a tank down by the pier but when the explosion died away it had gone. Safari claimed to be the only submarine which had torpedoed a tank on dry land.

Extract from 'One Man Band' by kind permission of Ben Bryant

Commander Ben Bryant, P.O. TGM McIntyre, Lt. B. Larkin.

J. H. Capes

John Hawtrey Capes was born on the 20th September, 1910, the son of an engineer/archaeologist/diplomat. We know little of John's early life except that he was educated at Dulwich College, a well known public school. He entered the Royal Navy rather late in his life. He was nearly 25 years old when he joined as a Stoker 2nd Class, on 20th May, 1935 (Most RN entrants are teenagers). He volunteered for the Submarine Service at the earliest opportunity (three years General Service having to be served in those days to qualify for 'Boats'). He started training in June 1938 and joined his first boat, the Submarine L 34 on the 18th of July that year.

After a period in spare crew he was drafted to the Submarine Olympus in October 1938, at that time attached to the depot ship HMS Medway on the China Station. On the 14th March, 1941, he was back in Dolphin joining the submarine Thrasher which heads off to the Middle East and is attached to Medway in Alexandria. During an earlier time in Malta, John (a keen motorist) had been in an accident while driving a hired car, he had collided with a horse-drawn vehicle and demolished it. His presence was required in Malta to settle with the 'Carossi' owner and arrangements were made for his passage to the island, now under siege, by what was known as the 'Magic Carpet Service' (submarines delivering stores, aircraft, spirit, ammunition and weapons from Alexandria and Gibraltar). He left Malta a few weeks later taking passage on the submarine Perseus which was leaving for patrol and would dock in Alexandria after that operation. John related to a newspaper, some thirty years later, that sacks of gold and silver plate were loaded onto the boat in the dark of night by officers of the Perseus and stored in the magazine (Malta was on the verge of being invaded at that time and I have not been able to obtain further information on this story. KTN-B). Perseus hit a mine* on 6th December 1941 (the eve of Pearl Harbour) and went down in 60 fathoms off Greece. John was the only survivor.

* Perhaps sunk by Italian Submarine 'Enrico Toti'

Signals Relating To Capes

C IN C LEVANT
(R) F O (S), S. 5,
S. O. (I) LEVANT

MOST SECRET

Your 1601/16 paragraph 2 and 1527/23 not to all addresses.

Stoker JOHN H. CAPES originally in THRASHER but later drafted to PERSEUS. Father almost certainly living in CAIRO. Rough description as follows:- Naval rating,
5 foot 10, dark, medium build, age approximately between 23 and 28, educated Dawlish College, well spoken. This rating when in THRASHER was granted leave to see his father in CAIRO.

= 1 1 4 6 B / 2 6

Ref. 1606/16: Survivor from PERSEUS believed to be in hiding with friendly Greeks.
1527/23: Not held.

NC-C TOR 0455 27.3.43.

Distribution: FO(S) DSO CSOO SOO SOI SEC SOA DAO

To: ADMIRALTY
from: C IN C LEVANT
(R) S.1 S.5 F.O.S.
S.O.I. ISTANBUL, S.O.I. LEVANT
COMBRAX PORTSMOUTH

DEFERRED
SECRET CYPHER

Reference my 161606B March not to Combrax Portsmouth and S.1's 261146B March not to admiralty and Combrax Portsmouth.
Rating ex PERSEUS is stoker JOHN H. CATES P/KX 86067 (not CAPES) as signalled in
S. 1's 311507B December 1941 not to all addresees. Rating was originally in THRASHER and later drafted to PERSEUS.
(2) MR. CATES almost certainly rating's father, a civil engineer resident in Cairo states he recieved letter from Combrax Portsmouth saying his son was missing presumed killed on 28th May, 1942, number in letter agrees with that in S. 1's 311507 December 1941.
(3) Next of kin has not yet been officialy informed.

0 2.1 1 1 6 C

Royal Naval Barracks,
Portsmouth,
14th May 1943

Dear Madam,

I am directed by my Lords Commissioners of the Admiralty to inform you that from information recently received at the Admiralty it is evident that at least one, and possibly four other members of the company of H. M. Submarine Perseus, survived the loss of the vessel in December, 1941 and is now being sheltered in enemy-occupied territory.

No information as to the identity of the survivors has been recieved and it is not known whether they are Officers or men or both.

In these circumstances my Lords have decided that the formal presumption of death of your son, John H. Capes, Stoker First Class, P/KX.86067, is to be rescinded and he will accordingly be regarded as missing pending the receipt of more definite information.

All possible steps are being taken to ascertain the number of survivors and their identities, but in order that their survival may remain a secret and so preserve them from falling into enemy hands the enquiries are being made with the utmost caution and secrecy and a long period will probably elapse before any definite news can be recieved.

I am, therefore, to request that you will maintain the strictest secrecy with regards to the information now imparted to you and communicate it only to those within your immediate family circle. Should any news of these men reach enemy ears their lives and those of their rescuers would be imperilled.

I am to add that any further information received will be immediately communicated to you and in the interests of all concerned to request that you will not write to me or the Admiralty on this subject.

Yours sincerely,

COMMODORE

Mrs. M. H. Capes,
'Noglands',
Chichester Road,
Emsworth,
Hants.

4 Part Serial - Salute The Submariner
By J. H. Capes - Petty Officer B.E.M. R.N. (Rtd.)

This is a true story of myself. What occurred is fact. I have been deliberately vague regarding the happenings on the island. The people who sheltered me undoubtedly saved my life at immense risk to themselves.

1. Mined! 2. Miracle escape. 3. Cephalonia. 4. Freedom.

Map of Area

This document was given to the editors (all ex-submariners) by the daughter of John Capes, we reproduce it exactly as it is related.

Part One

By the end of 1941 bomb shattered Malta had already stood 18 months of siege. All supplies had to cross about a thousand miles of hostile Mediterranean, coming from either Gibraltar or Egypt. But only sixty miles away was enemy Sicily and the German Air Force. Their main target was Malta's Manoel Island, the base of a handful of astonishingly successful British Submarines.

Here in the Vernon Club, at the top of the Baracca lift facing the Grand Harbour, I was in a small bar sampling a noggin of the local brew. A compatriot from the base, on passing, said there was a draft chit in the mess waiting for me. "This is it" I thought. On returning I had a quick peek on the table in the drawing office. There I saw a memo from the Commander (E) to Engineering Officer H. M. S. Medway about me. "Am sending you a peculiar animal. His antics are well worth watching", it said.

Twenty four hours later I found myself a passenger in H. M. Submarine Perseus, at sea, bound for patrol and Alexandria where I expected I would rejoin Thrasher, my old boat. Making myself a snug billet in an empty torpedo rack in the after ends of the Perseus, I shared a small tapering with two torpedo tubes embedded in a mass of operating machinery. Almost above me was a neat round escape hatch in the hull.

Three days brought us to the patrol area and the captain, Lieutenant Nickolay, gallantly took the boat through the mined waters between the Greek islands of Cephalonia and Zante. In the vicinity of Cape Glarenza, he successfully torpedoed and sank an enemy supply ship caught sneaking along the coast. Normally the crew knew little of attacks and their whereabouts, but I being periscope stoker at action stations was naturally aware of the events as they occurred.

The next night Perseus patrolled off Argostoli on the surface, very dark and windy. 'Up spirits' had just been piped over the tannoy speaker. It was 10 p.m. 7th December, 1941*.

The eventful night of the destruction of Pearl Harbour. I had saved some rum tots in my private blitz (Bottle). Tots kept me awake at night so I saved them for our return to harbour. That bottle turned out to be a lifesaver. I leaned back in my comfortable torpedo tray browsing over elderly letters.

* Officially 6th December 1941 in all reports on Perseus loss, KTN-B.

Suddenly a devastating explosion rocked the boat from stem to stern. My makeshift bed reared up throwing me in a complete somersault on to the deck... or what I thought to be the deck. The lights went out but not before I realised that the real deck was standing up and that I had been tossed on the forward bulkhead, normally a vertical wall of steel. I knew that Perseus was plunging to the bottom in a nose dive.
The bows hit the bottom with a nerve shattering jolt, the boat hung poised for a moment, standing on her head. Then the stern, where I was, fell back settling on the sea bed, possibly forever. Finally, the boat lay stretched on the uneven sea bed, listing almost 30 degrees on the Starboard side, the stern was now lower than the bows.
I guessed we had hit a mine, but by some miracle the after compartments were not yet flooded, and by another miracle, I was still alive, although the thump of hitting the bulkhead on my backside was very painful. No time for pains now. How about the chaps in the engine room? I groped for the torch near the escape hatch, "Thank Heaven", I thought, it was in it's position, and it worked! The powerful rays pierced the dank foggy air already beginning to stink of paint pouring from an upturned drum. The bulkhead on which I was tossed was more or less vertical again.
Through the watertight door, I went forrard, searching the stokers mess deck, then the bulkhead to the motor room. Electricians had apparently been killed by falling on live switches. As the rays fingered through the gloom of the engine room they revealed a ghastly sight, half of the cylinder heads at the front end of the engines had sheared off from the studs, with the operation gear hurled against the engine room forrard, thrown there by the sudden jerk of the last dive.
Beyond them was the bulkhead door, shut... but not by human hands. No clips had been secured. It must have been slammed by the first blast of the explosion, and was now held in place by water... crushing on the other side. It was creaking under the great pressure. Jets and trickles from the rubber joint seeped through. That door saved me and the three injured men I found alive in the debris. Our plight was one of vital horror. The water was rising in the engine room bilges and we were surrounded by the mangled bodies of a dozen dead. Perseus had become a cold steel tomb surrounded by the relentless sea.
With the cold already gnawing into me I thought of the rum in my blitz bottle. That would warm us up all right. I nipped back aft, had a stiff livener and handed the bottle round for a swift pick-me-up. I didn't

dwell on the very doubtful chance of escape. So far so good. I was still alive in one piece. My immediate thought was to help the others. One by one I guided them to the stern compartment. No time to be fussy about wounds. There was only one thing to do... to get out. The next problem was somehow to flood up the after compartment and get the men through to surface, if by luck nothing had fallen on the escape hatch to jam it.
Willing or not, in pain or not, dragged them aft to the escape hatch. Had the explosion warped it? Would the heavy list of the boat prevent it opening??? I didn't know, but would jolly soon find out. The depth gauge, if still functioning, showed a little over two seventy feet, that had to be overcome anyhow. No one as far as I knew, had ever attempted anything like it. I didn't give it further thought. If death was going to claim me it would not be without a fight.

Part Two

Irrepairably damaged, H. M. Submarine Perseus lay on the bottom of the Mediterranean, about 270 feet below a deadly minefield. Her forrard compartments, presumably flooded, listed to starboard almost 30 degrees.
It took half an hour to drag three wounded shipmates to the after escape compartment. By the light of my torch I gave them another noggin of rum each and had two myself. Liquor at least kept out the damp cold for the moment. The boat was leaking and would soon be flooded throughout. No time to waste. I shut the after water-tight door, isolating us in the stern compartment. I broke the seals of the four lockers and strapped the rubber escape sets on my companions. This device consists of a rubber lung, worn on the chest, a small bottle of high pressure oxygen across the stomach, a nose clip, goggles and a tightly fitting mouthpiece with adjustable rubber band around the neck, securing fairly comfortably. I soon had our sets in place. The atmosphere in this small space was becoming foul. I lowered the collapsible canvas trunk from a recess fitted around the escape hatch, and secured it by lashings to the deck. At the top of the trunk inside was the escape hatch, with four nuts holding four large clips securing the hatch firmly on th rubber seating joints all round the rim.
Reminding them of the drill, I found the valve in the most suitable position to flood the compartment from sea. I knew the water would rise

around the escape trunk, leaving a small space of air considerably compressed. This would stop the water rising further. Then we would have to insert our mouthpieces, duck down under the water coming up into the trunk and then out into the open sea through the escape hatch. The first job was to open the hatch, then return to the compartment to see the lads out. I found valve in starboard bilge, but the spindle was bent and immovable, we were trapped. If I could not move it, no one could. Was there an alternative?

If there was, it had to be found quickly before we were all frozen to death. Torpedo tubes? Could I flood them into the compartment by opening the front and back doors? I pondered but decided that as the hydraulic tele-motor system had lost all pressure this would be impossible. What else then? The under water gun! That was it. Thank god we were in the compartment with the gun in position in the lowest part of the compartment. This was normally used to send smoke signals to the surface for instruction purposes. It had four inch bore for rapid flooding. I knew the drill book advised us to avoid rapid flooding so we would have time to get used to the pressure gradually, but I had to chance it, we were waist deep now and the water was rising steadily, the only chance was to flood quickly, release the hatch and leave without a minutes delay. I splashed down to the gun and opened the breech, I tried the sluice valve gently and could feel the thrust of water entering. It increased to a steady whirl as the sea gushed in and then steadied, the air space round the hatch diminished rapidly. Here it came... the sea that would save us, drown us or freeze us to death.

Almost three hundred feet above, a strong wind was passing over a short choppy sea. As the water swirled around us almost chest high, a thick oily scum of paint spread itself across the dark swell in the small confined space. We still breathed this putrid air, slightly warmer from its own compression. I swiftly fitted my mouthpiece, settled on the nose clip and manipulated the needle valve on the oxygen bottle, flat across my stomach. I opened the mouthpiece cock and oxygen flowed into my lungs. Oxygen, the life saver, and at the same time, a killer. To breathe this gas under a pressure of fifteen atmospheres was risking oxygen poisoning in a matter of a few minutes.

Breathing painfully, I ducked down through the paint scum, groped for the bottom rim of the escape trunk, braced myself against the slippery angle of the deck and dragged myself upwards. Suddenly I found my head above water in the little pocket of air in the air lock below the hatch itself. I stretched out a hand and unscrewed the small vent cock in the centre of the steel lid. The air whistled out to the sea above, the slimy water rose above my face. My teeth were chattering, I realised the oxygen would not give me long.. I had much to do still. Using all my weight, I put my remaining strength on the tommy bar in the tube spanner to undo the dog nuts. Fortunately they were not corroded with salt and came away without difficulty. The vital moment came as the last nut dropped below me as I gave a mighty heave. The hatch flew wide open, a giant bubble of air escaped. I clung to the top rungs and rim of the hatch. I was free to ascend. I lost my mouthpiece, but managed to recover it and stuffed it back. Breath came again, and a few bubbles from the lung streamed upward.

The battle was almost won. I pulled myself back down, bobbed out from under the bottom of the trunk and poked my head into the foul air still trapped in the roof of the compartment... My torch showed the others to be still breathing...Quick now - first one bobbed down and out, next one, and a third, all gone. All now on their way to the surface, rising slowly through the freezing black water. Not too quickly or lungs would burst. I rubbed my goggles and dipped into the trunk for the last time. On coming out of the hatch, I felt over-head for the jumping wire, it had apparently snapped and fallen away. I flashed the torch around but was unable to see further than a few feet of rear casing steel deck, this was my last glimpse of the valiant Perseus.

I let go, the buoyant oxygen lifted me quickly upward. Suddenly I was alone in the middle of the great ocean with only a torch... that faithful steel torch... to make a friendly glimmer on the scene. The pain became frantic, my lungs and whole body was fit to burst apart. Agony made me dizzy. I realised I was coming up too quickly, so I unrolled the small apron and held it out in front of me, designed to act like a parachute in reverse. Theoretically, it was supposed to trap the water and slow the ascent, in fact all it did was to unbalance me and tip me head over heels. I let go and became upright again. The torch illuminated dirty looking wires, one brushed close, I passed a large cylindrical object. Wires hanging from it were caught in the light of my torch. I tried to hold my breath, but felt like a balloon about to burst. Dear God! How long can I last? A prayer was a natural suffix. With the suddenness of certainty, I burst to the surface and wallowed in a slight swell with whitecaps here and there. Had I returned to the land of the living? But where was this land?

Part Three

On reaching the surface after my miracle escape from around 270 feet, my first thought was for my companions. Having left the boat they should have survived the ascent as I did. Therefore they should be near me. Adjusting the set by shutting off the mouthpiece, I made the oxygen bag into a kind of lifebelt. I removed the nose-clip and lifted my goggles to have a good look round. The sea was choppy, whipped up by the wind and hardly ideal for swimming. My eyes followed the wave tops in the vicinity in a search of despair. There was nothing in sight. But what about the others? Had they all died in that last choking bid for the surface? Then, at some distance, I saw a ribbon of white, bobbing about on the wave crests. It appeared to be a broken line of cliffs. It was some distance away, possibly ten miles, could I manage a swim of that distance without any form of preparation and no food for hours?
Well I had survived this far and there was no stopping now...initially, one goal had been in sight... the surface. Now it had changed to land, however far away. Perhaps I was going to live... had always been going to live. Maybe the others had already struck out in the general direction. Although the night air had refreshed me, I knew I would not last for long in the present circumstances. I had to start swimming immediately so I tucked the cumbersome torch in my overall pocket and set out in a steady crawl. The torch proved a nuisance, it was heavy and awkward. It had been handy, but was only slowing me down now. Its beam was still on as I relinquished it and watched it drop towards the sea bed. Less encumbered, I made better progress, although the spray continually battered my face, I never lost faith. The will to live kept me going. Hour after hour I kept going, now on my back, now breast stroke, resting frequently. At last came the realisation that the land was closer. I could see the cliff formations clearer. In the background a high mountain loomed up. With renewed effort I plodded on, happy that there were no currents to negate my progress. This was the morning the sun revealed to a shocked world the devastation caused by Japanese treachery at Pearl Harbour. But to me, an almost insensible man paddling towards safety, it brought hope.
My mind, body and whole being were concentrated on one thing only... the shore. After an age of further endeavour, land and low pebbly beach came in sight. Almost within reach. As I approached the low cliff, the wind suddenly dropped. High above me, a line of rocks sloped seaward

to be washed by the restless waves. Steady now! not far to go, possibly fifty yards, my toe struck something hard. I paddled forwards to the rocks. I clutched solid rock. Gasping in dry air, I dragged myself upward, inch by inch, and eventually passed over the rocks onto a sandy beach. I crawled still further out of reach of the sea, under the frowning cliff, out of wind and weather, face down, head on hands, I lapsed into oblivion. When I awoke the sun was high in the sky, and I judged it to be about midday. Another thought struck me, and had to be tackled forthwith. Had I gained the land to become... a prisoner? Cautiously, I looked round me, raised my eyes to the cliff top and my hopes sank. Against the skyline stood an armed sentry gazing out to sea! and he wasn't one of ours.

Part Four

I lay completely exhausted in a sandy spot on the foreshore of the Greek island of Cephalonia in the Ionian Sea. My incredible nightmare escape from the sunken Perseus and a ten mile swim in December were over. High above me in the distance, on top of a steep shelving cliff, an enemy sentry gazed seaward. He appeared to be an Italian. Suddenly voices came to me. Two men slithering down a cleft concealed from the sentry. They bent over me, finding me alive, dragged me into a kind of small cave nearby. In fierce whispers they asked "Inglese? Inglese?" I nodded. They signalled me to stay put and ran back up the cleft like mountain goats. Later other villagers arrived, the first thing they gave me was a natural gourd containing Oozo, a firey local drink similar to anisette. It gave me an immediate warm glow. I accepted from them an odd jacket and trousers and khaki overcoat.

The village mayor arrived. With the help of an English dictionary, he explained that I had a choice. I could give myself up as a prisoner, or hide. I decided to hide if possible. If I had known the tremendous risk involved in this, I might have decided otherwise. By helping me the whole village placed themselves under pain of instant death. All justice had been hounded out of Greece. On Nazi orders from Athens, the invaders would think nothing of burning a house to the ground, its occupants locked inside, if known to have assisted spies. Sometimes whole villages were burnt to the ground!

That night a party from the nearest village returned, and I was lifted onto a small, elderly donkey, steered precariously up the cliff path.

Eventually, after passing between many stone walls, I reached a very small and I thought, extremely primitive dwelling. A few days later, the leaders of the village brought a man who turned out to be an agent of the underground movement. These valiant islanders were forever fighting their enemies. The agent promised that the underground would take care of me and perhaps arrange my escape.

Triumphantly, I wrote on a postcard... All well...Hawtrey. (My private name known only to a handful). I addressed it to Emsworth 369 my mother's telephone number. Many months later, in far away Hampshire, Mum mourned the loss of her son, already notified officially by the Naval Authorities. Through the letterbox, one morning, there fluttered a dirty dog eared envelope. Phone number traced and duly forwarded from bomb-torn Portsmouth depot. Unbelievably the message in someone's pocket evaded the stringent Nazi frontiers, brought joy to a mother's heart! Mum turned it over to the R. N. Signals buzzed. The unseen forces of the Resistance in Greece were put in motion, slowly but surely to get me out.

My life became one of desperation and boredom, mingled with the ever present fear of capture; and of course the reprisals taken against the people sheltering me would be obvious. The thirty mile long island was heavily garrisoned. I never stayed long in one place at all. Clandestine flights through the rugged countryside constantly took place. In the pitch dark on one of these escapades, I fell and rolled all the way to the bottom of a rocky ravine. I lost one of my important possessions, a small piece of soap. I now looked quite different, my appearance was altered. With hair dyed black and a Hitler moustache, I looked what I had to be... a half starved labourer in a down trodden impoverished land. I learnt the Greek dictionary pretty well by heart. I conversed only with my protectors as my pronunciation would give me away if I risked conversation with anyone else. There was always the risk of betrayal as a reward would certainly be exchanged for my capture.

Yet even when I was betrayed (not by a Greek) by a babbling fool woman, it only caused me further inconvenience. Always, at the moment of despair, some utterly poor but friendly and patriotic islander would risk the lives of all his family for my sake. They even gave me one of their prize possessions, a donkey called 'Mareeka'. There was a condition attached to her.

I had to take a solemn vow not to eat Mareeka. Often we would take to the mountain, fleeing from the enemy foraging in the vicinity. The main

advantage of this, was that it helped me to look the part completely. Many a time the donkey stubbornly refused to budge and sat down in mulish resentment at being taken from good grass to rock strewn mountain sides and various small caves, known only to a few indeed. By this time I had lost about five stones in weight. In some primitive surroundings I only had boiled roots and grass in severe circumstances. At times, I would have gladly left the donkey to her own devices, rather than drag the reluctant beast around in my everlasting wanderings. Nevertheless, she was really my faithful friend. Obviously nothing could appear more natural than an ill-clad peasant belabouring a scraggy beast of burden. In the course of my stay on the island, I was spoken to only once by an Italian sentry, who asked me for a match. I naturally produced it in stoney silence. This was the villagers natural attitude and consequently would prompt no suspicious thoughts. One of the more pleasant houses I stayed in had a large snow white tom cat... He was definitely patriotic. Through a chink in a shuttered part of the house I watched him sidle up to an Italian officer, in gorgeous uniform and jack boots. He stopped for a moment in the village pathway and looked around, possibly estimating the abode of pussy for a night capture for the pot. At this moment Pussy had the impertinence to soil those glossy boots. A shouted curse, out came the Beretta automatic, swift but inaccurate shots followed as Pussy bounded away to safety.
Eighteen long, solitary and anxious months passed before the dawn of the great day. Any plans for my safety or possible escape were kept a secret from me. This was a precaution to ensure I could give nothing away if captured. Milo, a weather-beaten fisherman, slouched into a small unoccupied house I had taken to the previous night. His small half decked schooner... only 25 feet long... was intended to carry me to freedom. First the boat had to go to Argostili to obtain a permit to carry local stores to enemy headquarters in Piraeus. The journey was meant to be made direct but Milo intended to creep round the coast and pick me up with two companions, off to join the Free Greek Forces at a secret rendezvous.
Milo had trouble at Argostoli. Three prospective Italian deserters got wind of his permit and demanded a trip to Athens. This was most serious. There was little room and, anyway, Milo was not going to Piraeus. He used guile and, fawning over his unwelcome guests, with copious drafts of Oozo made them drunk at a farewell party. Then they were flung into the fore-end cockpit and hatch battened down. Course was set

for the point where we waited in hiding for the pick-up.
We heard an engine... a powerful one. Obviously a torpedo boat. Slowly she passed the hiding place, the crew scanning the area through binoculars. I held my breath, fearful to be caught at the last gasp! Was this a coincidence or had someone given me away after all this time. I will never know. God was kind. The enemy vessel continued unsuspecting on her way. Later, Milo's boat chugged round the headland. With born skill, he came alongside a sloping jetty going into the water, largely sheltered by an overhanging ledge. Pent up with excitement we all jumped aboard. One of my companions fell in the sea but was fished out and hauled over the gunnel into the boat. One of the crew wiped up the bloodstains, the Italians had vanished!
Before us lay a journey of at least five hundred miles, the whole route infested with enemy held islands, whose coastal waters were patrolled by Italian vessels whilst overhead Nazi planes flew, menacing in the skies. Incidentally. Milo had been issued with a small pennant to fly at masthead, signifying he was on official business. At night he steered, wary for the speedy bow wave of a hostile craft in the vicinity. I was snugly concealed in a canvas bunk between two bulkheads. Very difficult to find without careful measurements being taken. By day Milo slept while we took the tiller. Once an aircraft zoomed round us and then sheered off. I did a sudden dive down the cockpit. When patrol vessels and shore batteries had been passed all but Milo kept hearts in mouths. We were not molested in any way although the weather lashed the little boat with unexpected gales. Donkey meat was our diet and black bread of very doubtful origin. Mareeka had been returned at the last moment, I am glad to say.
Six days had now passed. The Aegean crossing had been made and the faithful schooner chugged its way peacefully through the long approaches to the Turkish Harbour of Smyrna, where we anchored off the ruins of a town demolished by earthquake. "Ianny" cried Milo, "Quick, take a swim and wash. Somebody important is coming to see you". I dived overboard, a few quick strokes, and clambered back aboard. I was struggling back into my old clothes as a launch came alongside. On her deck stood a neat figure in glistening tropical whites... waving a flask of brandy. The British Consul himself, immaculate to the monnacle! "Oh! my poor boy how <u>do</u> you feel?".
I had come through this most hazardous escape unharmed. If there is a moral to this story it is **NEVER SAY DIE**.

Official Report

Citation by Capt. S. 1 'Medway II' 14/7/43

"This rating was in the after end of the PERSEUS when she was sunk, apparently by a mine off Cephalonia on 6/12/41. By great courage, perseverance and calm judgement, he effected an escape by the DSEA under what must have been most trying conditions, which is as successful an attempt as has ever been made as he must have been considerably shaken; so great had been the force of the explosion of the mine that all but 5 of the crew were apparently killed almost instantaneously. The submarine sank bow down at an almost perpendicular angle and she was lying on the bottom heeled to starboard. After making good his escape from the submarine, he swam ashore and was looked after by the Greeks. Largely helped by his own skill, tenacity and perseverance, he succeeded in escaping."

<u>Most Secret undated and unsigned Report in docket (? by De-Briefer)</u>

Capes embarked in the P at Malta on 24/11/41 and left on an operational trip in the Aegean. It was intended that this should end at Alexandria. The submarine went into action at dawn on 3rd Dec., firing 2 torpedoes and Capes believes that targets were hit. The patrol was then continued towards Cephalonia.

At 2200 on 6th Dec. there was a terrific explosion which C believes was caused by a mine. All starboard ballast was lost and the sub assumed an angle of 90 degrees. She sank rapidly and touched bottom, bow first at a perpendicular angle. Finally, she settled full length on the seabed, still retaining a big starboard angle. Capes was standing on the steering wheel (sic) in the after end and from some object he recieved a considerable blow on the posterior.

Every pipeline and valve in the after end and rear compartments were broken. All lighting failed within 15 seconds of the explosion. Capes found that of the crew of 55 only 5 besides himself were still alive after the sub had settled - no officers, petty officers or seamen other than five other stokers, all from the after end and rear compartments. They must have been killed by the explosion and subsequent flooding.

Eventually, 2 lamps of the secondary lighting system were found and switched on and the D.S.E.A. equipment got out of the lockers and donned. The sub was then flooded by means of the underwater gun (?) the water rising rapidly to about 3fi - 4ft. The hatch trunking was then pulled down. A pipe was disconnected from the high pressure airline and the valve cracked slightly open to allow air to enter the after air compartment. It was felt that the compartment would become flooded without chance of escape since water was rising rapidly owing to the punctures in the exterior hull. The DSEA hatch clips were taken off and the trunking then attached to the deck. All this was very difficult to accomplish, the starboard ship's side being used as the deck and the fact that a drum of oil and one of enamel had burst and greased the water made it hard to keep the DSEA nose clips on.
At this point, only one other stoker remained and the sub re-settled itself on the bottom taking a still more acute starboard angle. Pressure on Z tank first showed 60lbs but on the sub re-settling, the gauge was on full stop, showing 70lbs or more.
Capes tried to leave with the DSEA torch but owing to the blast of air coming through the DSEA canvas trunking, he was forced to return to the compartment. He refitted his nose-piece etc. and re-entered. The outside hatch jumping wire was not visible and he proceeded slowly to surface. The DSEA apron controlled his speed very efficiently and the time taken to ascend was about 1fi minutes. A few feet from the surface he saw a mine about 10 - 15 feet away.
On surfacing, he signalled SOS with the torch towards the land but there was no answer and no sign of other survivors. He thought the time that had elapsed since the explosion was about 1fi hours. He began to swim to the shore about 5 - 6 miles away and reached the shore at dawn, some six hours later. He was very weak and fearful lest a sentry he saw on a hill about half a mile away should have seen him, but he managed to reach a small cave unobserved.
At 1000, two villagers entered the cave and were surprised to see him but after some discussion (?) one of them left and returned bringing some dry clothes. They then dug a shallow hole in which he lay hidden until nightfall. At night he was moved by donkey to the village of Mavrata, about 2 miles away. Here in the house of Gerasimos Vallianos he stayed for fourteen days. The villagers were generally suspicious of Capes, thinking him a German spy, but he was well treated and a doctor was fetched to him.

In addition to Vallianos, two brothers named Shokas were very helpful. At the end of the fourteen days, Capes was sufficiently recovered to make the journey on foot of three miles to Hionata escorted by Vallianos. He remained at Hionata for four days in the house of a family who would not reveal their name. On the fourth day Italians came to the house of Nicolas Haldas where he stayed for two days. On the seventh day in Hionata, Capes was taken by car to the house of Yianni Kritikos in Rosata, about 20 miles from Hionata. The same evening he went on foot to Pharaklata and stayed in the house of Yianni Pollatos.

On 24th December, the Italians came to occupy the village and Capes left on foot escorted by Cleo Pollatos. After walking 3 miles, they were met by Evangelatos in a car and driven to Kourouklata where Capes stayed for twenty days in the house of Phillipos Bosigos and a further ten days in another part of the village.

At the end of January 1942, Capes was moved to the house of Hellene Kosmetatos in Minies. Here he was very well looked after as Mmme. Kosmetatos was English. She was also fairly rich and provided him with clothes and food during the greater part of his stay in Greece. He stayed at her house for twenty days and during this time, the Regia Marina sent an investigation party with the Greek spy Kondamikalos to look for oil in the house. But Mr. Koss succeeded in keeping Kondas from searching the upper floors of the house and the Italians did not question Capes' presence there.

At the beginning of July, Capes left for Argostoli and stayed one night at the house of Gerasimos Razis, who proved very helpful both then and over a period of many months. In the morning, he left for Keramies (?) staying twenty days in the house of George Metaxas. On the arrival of an Italian patrol, Capes left Keramies for Rosata and stayed with Kritikos during August and September 1942. At this time it was heard that Yianni Gimis of Argostoli had been seized by the Carabinieri for possessing a radio. Since Gimis was naturally indiscreet and it was known that the Carabinieri used brutal methods of torture, it was feared that Gimis might betray Capes; so he left for the Pollatos home in Pharaklata. Here he stayed for five days eventually leaving for Sematata where he lived with Vangelis Thomatos (?). During his stay in Semtata, on the 14th October from a hill overlooking the sea, Capes saw the conning tower of a British submarine.

After a month in Semtata, Capes left for Metaxala (?) and stayed until the 10th December in the house of Nicolas Metaxas.

On the 10th he went again to Pharaklata, this time on horseback and stayed until the middle of January, 1943 with Pollatos. Then he was removed to a house owned by Kritikos in Argostoli. Food was now becoming scarce and Capes and his helpers were reduced to eating roots and herbs as all normal food had been seized by the invaders.
Meat and corn were forbidden to the people and obtainable only on the Black Market at prohibitive prices. Capes noticed the brutality of the Carabinieri who were the most vicious of the Italian garrison.
On the 5th February, Kritikos's father was seized by the Carabinieri for supposedly Communist activities, and due to this fact and the fact that Madame Kritikos was indisposed, Capes left alone for Pharaklata. Here he stayed until 4th April, 1943. He was then fetched by Cleo Pollatos to the house of Vangelis Pillarinos on the main street of Argostoli. On 25th May, Cleo came to the house and told Capes he would be leaving Cephalonia as she understood arrangements had been made for his escape.
On 26th May, he was taken to the house of George Metaxas where an unknown Greek showed him a note from Major Parrish (?). On 27th he was taken by car to Poros with Cleo, Metaxas and his wife and a further unknown man. Outside Poros Capes was met by Gerasimos Vanthoros and introduced to Evangelatos and Captain Milton who passed on to Capes details for his escape. In the early morning of the third day he was taken to an empty house overlooking the quay where he remained until 30th May. In the morning of the 30th he was taken to a small bay about three miles away by Vanthoros and his brother Nicolas. Sentries had been posted on a hill behind the bay and at each end of it to warn the escapers if the Italians came. At 0930 an Italian MAS boat swept round the headland and came close inshore at slow speed in the direction of Argostoli. Capes and his companions hid in the rocks and were not seen.
At 1000 a caique appeared and hove close to inshore. A boat was lowered from it and Capes and Nicolas Vanthoros were taken out to the caique, which then sailed and arrived safely at Kioste on 2nd June, 1943 after a 3 day voyage.

Capes was awarded the BEM, Suppt to the London Gazette 14/12/43.

Extract From Commendation For Decoration For Captain M. Houmas OBE.

Master Of The Greek Caique Evangelistria, By Brigadier D. A. Clarke, Commanding "A" Force In The Aegean 1944.

"In may 1943 he was selected to go to Cephalonia, on the west coast of Greece to pick up Stoker Capes, sole survivor of the submarine 'Perseus'. This involved a long trip through enemy waters under constant patrol from ships and aircraft. On arrival in Cephalonia he was given a detailed interrogation by the Italian Harbour Police. He managed to lull their suspicions regarding the irregularities of his arrival and lack of the necessary permits. Having landed an agent whose duty was to contact Capes, he was ordered by the Italians to another port. On arrival there his caique was boarded by Italian police. By adroit replies and bribery he contrived to maintain comparative freedom. Later he found it necessary to contact Capes himself, which entailed a long journey overland. Finally, in pursuance of a plan he had evolved to suit the exigencies of this particular situation, he returned in his caique to the original port where Capes was embarked, and although under observation, set sail for Turkey, where he arrived twelve days later, having completed a journey of 1,000 miles".

(Note: Houmas received the DSO).

Gus's Interview With Crash Cooke

Conversation with Crash Cooke on October 10th 1989. J. W. F. Cooke served on submarines from 1933 until 1959.
After the Medway sinking I was involved in setting up a base in Port Said. I was in Beirut as spare crew coxswain, then went to a transit camp in the desert somewhere near Cairo, I think. I was in charge of a group of submarine ratings going to England. I was allocated a tent, which was over a large pit dug into the ground. One day I was asleep or laying down on my bed... I was brought back to reality by a very strange laugh. I looked up and saw this man!... He said to me "Hello Crash, don't you remember me?"... "You remember me - I'm Johnny Capes - I was a survivor from Perseus". I said "I thought she was lost with all hands including my friend Reggie Meek, the coxswain". "The officer of the watch wants to see you" so I went over and saw him. He said "You have to keep this rating with me all the way to England". I took the draft to Port Tewfik. I received orders from presumably Captain S there that I had to deliver him personally to Captain S at Fort Blockhouse.
On the transport ship which went to Diego Suarez and then round the cape to Locerpool, he had the most insane laugh which upset many people. He had an educated voice... he told me the story of his escape from Perseus many times and the story never varied... it was word perfect. I am still convinced to this day that he was never ever on Perseus when she sailed. He said he was the only one in the after ends which I feel is strange... he told me he had been in Greece with the resistance. Unusually, his father lived in Cairo at the Turf Club. In the face of the evidence at the submarine museum, I am still convinced that Capes was not on Perseus.

GUS BRITTON: "I am equally sure that he was on Perseus because how could he have been in the area where the boat was sunk? Crash Cooke thinks that Capes was not on Perseus when it sailed and somehow got to Turkey where he was picked up. This is too much of a million-to-one chance happening. Impossible in fact. Capes was a Public School boy in the R. N. as a stoker, which is extraordinary in itself and the Perseus story was just another part of his bizarre life. I think that perhaps something happened in Perseus in the after ends that would have reflected on him... panic and fighting to escape or something like that."

Gus Britton
Asst. Director
Submarine Museum.

Letter To Gus Britton From Jim Warren

Hollingbourne,
Kent.

27th April, 1986

Dear Gus,
Firstly, I would like you to know that I have given up any idea for a memorial to the late Captain Sladen.
Now the reason for taking up your time. As you will see from the enclosed photocopy of a letter in the current S.O.C.A. News, our mysterious Capes has turned up, not altogether senile, but getting on that way and without home or family.
As the Trials Officer of the A.E.D.U., I had a little to do with the investigation for the Ruck Keene report on Submarine Escape, with Bill Shelford I had at least three sessions with Capes and each time his account of his escape from Perseus was different. A number of men were consulted such as D.S.E.A. Coxswains, Chief Stokers of "P" boats and the like. Whilst the drill was correct, what in general we did not believe was him going back to look after the others, but without any other survivors, we accepted his story.
I never knew the rest of history and, as you will see, on page 147 of Bill Shelford's 'Subsunk', at the time of publication - 1960 - there was some security on his activities from December, '41 until he turned up in '43 in Turkey.
Now all this is interesting but what is more so is that on Friday, I was having a lunch time session with Bill Curtis, who had just resigned as Chairman of the S.O.C.A. Medway branch. He was a Leading Seaman with me on Rover and I had a lot to do with him as a D.S.E.A. coxswain in Chariots. He had a job with the local Ministry of 'Ag. & Fish' and, to my surprise, turned up here to advise me on the welfare of my cattle. He obviously had not read the Stokers Manual! Anyway he told me more about Capes. Shortly after the War he, Curtis, was travelling North and in his compartment was an ex R.A.F. chap, they got talking and the R.A.F. chap asked Curtis if he knew Capes, he had been attached to an R.A.F. boat squadron in the Med. and he had been sent to land stores on an island and bring off Capes. When they arrived, there was no mistaking that Capes was in the reception party with an attractive Greek female.
Having turned over the stores they were about to leave when they discovered that two jars of rum and Capes with female, had vanished. The rum and girl are well within Capes' capacity.
Can I ask you for help? First, where can I find any papers dealing with the Ruck Keens report? Who could tell me if there is still any security on his absent two years? Have you any record? As you will know, in 'Broken Column', we did the story of A. B. Wilde. We went out to the area he worked in and got a first-hand account, in other words, we checked his story. I think I could do the same here. I have very good relations with the British School in Athens and have been to Turkey and have contacts there.
I shall be very grateful indeed for any advice or comments you care to give me.
Kind Regards.
Yours sincerely,
Jim Warren.

Hollingbourne,
Kent.

5th May, 1986

Dear Gus,
You have no idea how much I appreciated your many postcards - even if they weren't numbered, but being an ex-member of the more intelligent branch of the Andrew, I was able to sort them out. Sorry about the enclosure, but in case you have not seen the S.O.C.A. News, I enclose another and also a copy of a letter I have received from Sladen's Son. We shall be going to Scotland all going to plan this summer we stay at Universities, self catering if you want, cheap and no rig of the day, we shall go via Durisdeer and lay a wreath. As I expect you know they are going to lay up Trident's bell at Dursley in July. I shall try and go down. Thank you for your offer regards Capes, but I will leave it till I see you, which I am hoping will be during the week beginning May 26th, you choose a day when I can take you to a pint and eats. I would like to walk round the Fort, see the Chapel, the Grand Hotel and the Wardroom.
Now you are right about Capes but apart from his escape which could have been one of those things; he was somehow blown out, if it was a controlled escape, I find it hard to believe he was the only survivor, the mystery is why does he tell such a story? You may have read our "Broken Column", well we were put on to this story by Bromage who only gave us the bare outline. We found Wilde and he added a bit more and gave us the area and some contacts. We went to Italy and checked everything, if anything, Wilde underplayed his part. Now use this technique with Capes, give me a starting point, where did he land in Zante? And how did he get to Turkey? And most interesting, how did the R. A. F know where he was? I have good contacts with the British School in Athens so if there is any sort of Old Comrades of the Resistance, they'll put me on to it.
If you like it is personal interest, perhaps a short story with a question mark over what happened to the Perseus and his escape. I have written to Bill Bailey with S.A.E. asking if he would like a lunch time session, again a short story, "Where are they now". Talking to Bill Curtis the other day, we wondered if there was sufficient escape stories of Lower Deckers to make a book which could be sold for the Alliance Charity, what do you say? I knew of the Stratagem, yes - let's talk it over. I agree with you that Capes is not going to make the headlines, but there is something wrong, somewhere and, being the person I am, I would like to find out. I cannot get a publisher for my book, the trouble is it needs an editor and today publishers do not want to go to this expense. I do not want any advance, I want to tell my story of the Submarine Service which I knew and was very very proud to have served in. You can keep the Royal Navy, I hated it. Submarines I loved, can you imagine what going out to China in 1935 was like? And coming home in '37 (cost me 100 dollars) with Willie Banks as S.S.O. ? Dived every day to get 'tropics'. We were worth a fortune by the time we got to Blockhouse. I bought a car, an M.G. As a Killick Stoker, I lived like a lord up in Barrow standing by the Undine. I had saved quite a bit in China especially the last time we visited Shanghai where the market in French Letters was a 'sellers' - The Russian girls couldn't get enough and Charlie Jones our Coxswain couldn't understand our virility, ten times and more a night was going it, in his elderly mind, but he still coughed them up.
It was good practical experience for my business life after retirement.
All the best and my kindest regards to Jeannie and all of you.

Jim Warren

Conclusion

To describe John as enigmatic would be an understatement. He was a likeable rogue who would probably have been a pirate had he lived a couple of centuries earlier. I served with Johnny Capes for more than a year in submarines and found him to be very unconventional, disliking higher authority, and making that fact plain. An ex-public schoolboy, he was on a more elevated intellectual level than many of the Grammar School educated junior officers above him in our small service. Orders from his superiors usually came in the nature of a request. When I contacted John's daughter Julie for photographs of her father for this book, she replied that it would be hard to find one without a pint in his hand or a strange woman on his arm, or both. "That was the chap I knew!" but if you were in trouble, which was quite often if you went ashore with John, he was the best mate any young stoker could have.

John's exit from the sunken Perseus is one of the great submarine escape stories. A mine exploding only yards away, alone on the sea bed with the dead bodies of his mates in the only secure compartment left. The flooding up and getting out of the boat at 360 feet, with what was primitive equipment designed for escape of less than 100 feet. Swimming to shore, a distance of more than 7 miles with an injured buttock - Many could not believe that he had escaped from that depth and all kinds of stories circulated in the service. That he jumped out before sinking (Bill "Cutts" Curtis), that he was not aboard Perseus ("Crash" Cooke), because all boats had their hatches bolted down from outside except conning tower and gun hatch (to prevent lifting in the event of depth charging).

If we take Bill Curtis's theory, the after escape hatch would have to be of the central handwheel type for quick release, which it was not. I did check with the builders (Vickers) it was of the four dog type as Capes stated.

"Crash" Cooke thought that John was not on board and that he had deserted and found his way to Turkey where he was picked up. This could not be so - Gus Britton agreed that he must have been on Perseus.

The tale of the ex-R.A.F. Boat Squadron crew member from Jim Warren's letter to Gus Britton could be quite true. I knew from experience that women and rum were two of Johnny's weaknesses. He could have been feeling well attached to this female and not, at that time, wanted to be rescued.

Research in the years following the 1939-1945 War has shown that it is possible to survive the enormous pressure at depths of more than 100 fathoms but that is with intense training and the right conditions.
John's own story was written for a newspaper as a serial in four parts (it was never published). He can be excused for using some artistic licence in the story as it was for lay people who may not be able to read between the lines as a submariner would. The de-briefer's narrative to my mind is a fair reflection of the truth. Years later the wreck of Perseus was located by divers and was found to be as Capes related with the after hatch open.
This incident is given two pages in the book by Alastair Mars DSO DSC★ 'Submarines at War 1939-1945'. Mars was perhaps best qualified to comment on Capes' story as he had interviewed John on his return to England. In 1940 Mars had been the first Lt. of Perseus and knew the boat inside out. If anybody could have proved that Capes was fabricating his tale it was Mars, but he said at the time that Capes was a very brave man and I can only agree with him.
Our service is full of characters, our own President Rear Admiral Ben Bryant C.B. DSO★★ DSC is best known for his expert use of the gun. He probably sank more shipping by gun that any other submarine skipper. Others like VC's Linton, Wanklin and 'Gamp' Miers all had that certain charisma that made them stand out head and shoulders above their contempories. As with the lower deck, certain personalities emerge as ones to remember; Gordon Selby; Alfie Betts; 'Buckwheat' Harris; 'Diesel' Jones and many others but the best known 'skate' must be the one and only Johnny 'Choppa' Capes who was a legend in his own lifetime.

K. Nethercoate-Bryant

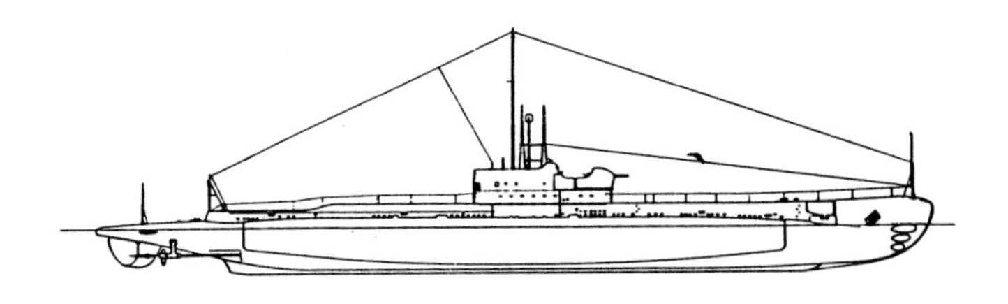

John Capes (Centre)

John Capes (Right)

Why He Was Called 'Crash'

There he goes... talking ten quid above his kit upkeep allowance! 'Crash' Cooke, also known as the 'Claw' (after shooting some fingers off while rabbiting), was coxswain of a boat running from Alexandria. The boat was outboard of the trot in Alex when the wardroom silver had to be mustered prior to taking it inboard to the depot ship. The coxswain's store you may remember was adjacent to the wardroom. 'Tanky' was down in the store while Cooke was up top with the muster list. "All right Tanky"... Twelve fish knives, (Always useful to make submarine brooches and tiepins*) 'crash' as manky old pussers knives went into the sack. "Twelve forks Tanky", 'crash' as twelve equally manky forks went into the sack. And so it went on. Eventually Tanky (well primed with 'bubbly') came out of the store onto the forecasing and proceeded to make his way over the brow. (Whether or not one of the slats had been deliberately loosened was a moot point). 'Crash' Cooke on the casing was urging Tanky to be careful when the inevitable happened... Over the side went Tanky and the 'wardroom silver', 'Crash' was jumping up and down on the casing, doing his best to win an 'Oscar'. It was said that the diver who went down subsequently was also well primed with bubbly. Alexandria harbour waters were very murky and nothing was ever recovered.

Dickie Elliot.

Dickie

* I made several submarine brooches (not I hasten to add, from wardroom fish knives although this was done often) as 'ground bait' when I was young and single, finally got round to making myself a tie pin, only to lose it going on draft. Many were fabricated using only a nail file, with hours of laborious work but I was more fortunate... I drew a set of pussers needle files!

H.M. Submarine Strongbow

H. M. Submarine Strongbow - 4th War Patrol

Commanding Officer-Lieutenant J. A. R. Troup DSC.

In Far Eastern Waters - 30/12/1944 - 19/1/1945.

H.M.S/M Strongbow sailed from H.M.S. Wolfe Trincomalee on 30th December 1944 our 'billet' being Zone "H" in the Malacca Strait which was south of Penang. The first five days were spent on passage doing the usual deep dive and dives each day for trim. On 6th January the patrol began and all was quiet until the 8th January. After sighting one target sighted a second which offered a better chance of interception. Aircraft forced boar to dive and the target was closed submerged. The boat then surfaced and opened fire. After firing some 20 rounds and obtaining 2 hits a large vessel southbound was sighted. This offered a better target so Strongbow broke off action and dived to await this new target. However this vessel must have scented trouble as it turned and steamed rapidly away. At dusk on 9th January a 2-4000 ton ship with two chasers as escorts was sighted and after plotting its course by Radar it seemed its apparent destination was Penang. Strongbow had three options, a night attack on the surface (weather conditions not being favourable for this), continuing to shadow and attack submerged at dawn or to proceed ahead to Penang and await target dived.

The third alternative was chosen and the boat dived about 06.00 off the southern entrance to Penang but enemy did not materialise. During the course of 10th January a junk was sunk by gunfire and in the late afternoon what appeared to be an innocent merchant ship some 10 miles away and which the Strongbow chased at full power, turned out to be a Japanese destroyer believed to be of the "WAKATAKE" class. The enemy had either sighted us or was using radar and closed in rapidly. We dived and shut off for depth charging. As she finally closed we went deep and she passed overhead dropping a pattern of six depth charges. It was thought at the time that no damage had been sustained but in view of what happened later there was strong suspicion that one of our fuel tanks had sprung a leak. We withdrew and eventually lost contact with H.E. The 11th and 12th January were quiet and we had no contact with the enemy.

On 13th January we dived at 05.25. At 06.00 we found ourselves in the middle of four enemy ships - two frigates (one 'Mikura' class) and two A/S vessels. The submarine was silenced as all four closed to attack.

Between the hours of 06.20 and 13.30 each of the four attacked from various angles when patterns of various numbers were dropped anything from three to five charges. No damage of a really serious nature was sustained during this period except that the boat was considerably shaken. However the Asdics had a defect on the training contacts forward and finally jammed altogether which made life very difficult for the Ping boys Len Ridge, Alex Morrison and George Lorimor but they did an excellent job in the adverse conditions. At just after 14.00 one of the four passed right overhead and dropped a pattern of three which were within an estimated 10 feet of the port engine and considerable damage was caused. All lights in the after ends went out and many elsewhere. The Sperry went off the board for the third and last time. The magnetic compass became obscure and the steering became erratic. The Asdic set blew up with a most spectacular flash. The After planes jumped 12 degrees out of line. The forward D.S.E.A. and Engine room hatches lifted and fortunately seated again. A heavy H.P. air leak developed behind the Chart Table and there were several big telemeter leaks and last but not least we lost trim. An interesting phenomenon was that of a cup and saucer on the Wardroom Table, these jumped about eight inches into the air, the saucer then disintegrated in mid air and the cup fell down again quite intact.

As a result of the loss of trim the boat hit bottom at 165 feet. The stern was down by about 20 degrees and everything was then shut off.

We then waited for the next attack everybody in the Control Room thinking the next would be the last as it was going to be impossible to take evasive action but it never came. Somewhere between 17.00 and 17.30 the Skipper decided that an attempt be made to get the boat off the bottom. In view of the stern being down all available hands were sent forward in case the screws were stuck but by using the pump and motors after some hesitation the boat came off the bottom up to periscope depth. The After Periscope was useless and the Forward Periscope had double vision in H.P. but was reasonable in Low Power although somewhat muzzy. It was found that there were still four vessels in the area and in view of the state of the forward periscope it was decided to go down to 90 ft and move away from the scene of the action as quietly as possible.

By this time the whole of the crew were completely exhausted in view of the intense heat which had built up during the course of the action.

Everyone was suffering from dehydration through lack of water and some, particularly in the Engine Room had great breathing difficulties one or two being virtually unconscious. In the Motor Room the temperature had reached 200 degrees and had to be evacuated*. The water pressure was lost early in the action so that each member of the crew had to survive on a few mouthfulls of water which Joe Blamey (E.O.) was able to obtain during one of the attacks and a small tin of orange juice for a period of 15 to 16 hours. Finally we surfaced at around 2000 hrs and proceeded south on Main Motors and after about an hour commenced running on main engines. In the first hour of the 14th January enemy vessels were sighted believed to be some or all of the original four. Dived for an hour or more. Eventually surfaced again and proceeded on main motors until felt safe to switch to Main Engines.
Dived shortly before 06.00. Unable to effect any improvement on both periscopes. The port shaft was making a considerable amount of noise and there had been a great deal of vibration from the port engine during the night. Various other problems were discovered including the movement of the Control Room deck as the ladder, instead of being at an angle, had become upright and the Conning Tower lids were damaged. Surfaced shortly after 18.00 when signal was transmitted giving brief details of damage sustained particularly periscopes. A number of problems were found in Engine Room and the Motor Room particularly on the port side. After about 4 hours recieved signal to leave patrol. 15th-18th January on passage. Carried out deep dive of 350ft which was a tense time but apart from a few leaks on the port side aft the boat held together.
19th January - Secured alongside H.M.S. Wolfe in Trincomalee. Shortly after the Strongbow was put into dry dock and it was no surprise to find interframe indentations along its port side abaft the engine room which accounted for the holding down bolts being bent and the engines misaligned. Also the rudder and after hydroplanes had been badly damaged by the tremendous pressure created by the depth charges. Nothing could be done about the hull except that 4" steel angle bars were welded to the interior of the hull to strengthen the worst places.

* As much as possible (This can be confirmed by Stan Biggs & Nobby Clark. Both still SOCA members).

All repair work which was considerable and extremely difficult in certain respects was carried out in the dry dock to make it fit for patrol again and eventually we were back alongside "Wolfe" where we took on repaired machinery and reconditioned periscopes. After which a report was sent to the higher authorities giving full details of the damage sustained and repairs carried out. In the meantime we carried out engine and motor trials which appeared be satisfactory but then we did a deep dive to 300ft.

When we reached a little over that depth a terrific column of water cascaded down from above just aft of the engine room bulkhead watertight door. The Skipper having witnessed the cascade had already ordered "Blow all main tanks". The 4" internal diameter bonded rubber insert (of which we had 6 fitted) in the cooling system had burst and the water pressure being in excess of 135 lbs per square inch at 300ft allowed a full flow of water. In the 45 seconds or thereabouts it took us to surface we took in something like 12 tons of water. As a result of the "bow up" angle when we surfaced all the water flowed aft but fortunately no damage was caused. As Joe Blamey said "Luckily we had our cooling system shut off during our recent depth charging or the pressure would certainly have burst them all".

After this we were preparing for the next patrol when a signal was recieved from the higher authorities ordering us to return to the U.K. so that a thorough check could be made to see if Strongbow was fit to carry out another full patrol.

However before returning to the U.K. in the operation to recapture Rangoon, Strongbow carried out a further patrol east of the Bay of Bengal. Also in the operation were "Scythian", "Statesman" and "Subtle" in the southern Malacca Strait and "Seadog" off the Tenasserim Coast. Strongbow carried out a weather reporting and air/sea rescue assignment which fortunately meant we surface ran other than trim dives. Apart from being a sitting duck on the surface for enemy aircraft or submarines the crew generally had little faith in the capabilities of the boat when submerged so it was happy relief when we returned to Trincomalee.

Shortly after we returned to the U.K. which was uneventful except that we had to stay over at Port Said as our First Lieutenant Mitchener had a bout of Malaria and the Skipper would not go without him. Fortunately as the European war was over we surface ran all the way. While at Port

Said the crew had some interesting runs ashore but that's another story. After a weekend at Blockhouse we went round to Chatham Dockyard where a full check on the boat was carried out during which time the crew got leave in two watches and while the second watch was on leave the Japanese unconditionally surrendered after the Atom bombs. Great relief as a second stint in the Far East was not a pleasant thought to most of the Strongbow's crew.

As a result of the check the boat was condemned as unfit for further service and subsequently after returning to Blockhouse was sent on to Falmouth with a skeleton crew to the breaker's yard.

The Captain had stated in his patrol report that it was quite a mystery how the 4 Japanese anti-submarine vessels held Strongbow for so long and then appeared to lose contact. On our return to the U. K. it was learnt from official sources that the Japanese had actually claimed the Strongbow as sunk*. There was a theory which went about the boat that as a result of the pattern of depth charges by the Japanese destroyer on 10th January 1945 one of the fuel tanks had been fractured thus causing a continuous leakage of oil. When the boat hit the sea bed a considerable amount of oil came to the surface and this was the reason for the Japs breaking off the attack and claiming that it had been sunk.

This always sounded a logical explanation but if this was not the case then those members of SOCA who were on Strongbow on its fourth patrol in the Far East all agree that our escape was a miracle.

While on leave it was announced that our Skipper now Lt. Commander Troup had been awarded a second D.S.C. Joe Blamey (E.O.) a D.S.C. to

* Jack Pollard married Joan on the 6th June 1942. Joan was 'aide' to a general in the War Office and saw secret information as it was recieved into that place. She relates the following..."I read a report in late January 1945 from the Naval, Air and Military situation at the time to the effect that the Japanese claimed H. M. Submarine STRONGBOW as sunk in that theatre of war" (Her colleagues had unsuccessfully tried to withhold this information from her knowing her husband was a crew member) "I never knew how I got through the rest of that day and the next few days before I recieved a telegram from Jack to say he was safe"

add to his D.S.M. awarded while on the "Porpoise" and 4 to 6 D.S.M.'s were awarded to the crew including Len Ridge as leading Asdic Operator plus two M.I.D.'s. Some years later our skipper rose to the rank of Vice Admiral Sir J. A. R. Troup KCB DSC★and did his stint as Flag Officer Submarines.

We did get some press coverage of the action but this was overshadowed by the surface action of "Shakespeare" in an adjacent billet roughly about the same time which made much more exciting reading though we suffered much more extensive damage.

The above is just a summary of the events which took place during the fourth patrol of Strongbow in the Far East and does not give the full details of the damage sustained by the boat during the main action on the 13th January, 1945. However, the fact that not withstanding the extensive repairs which were carried out at Trincomalee. the boat was condemned for further service after careful examination at Chatham Dockyard confirms such damage was much more serious than most had really suspected. It must be stated that certain member of the Engine Room crew were distinctly jumpy about doing another patrol on the boat and only got back to normal when we were on our way home to the U. K. and were not required to dive any more.

Finally, there is no doubt that all members of Strongbow's crew on the patrol who are still alive today will remember that epic 13th January, 1945 although it is now almost 48 years on and would agree that, dare it be said, our Boatmate up above or vice versa was keeping a good 'watch' over us that day.

JACK POLLARD
L/TEL. ON STRONGBOW 1943-1945

L to R: Lt. J. A. Troop DSC. (Captain), Sub Lt. G. McAlpine RNVR, Wt.Eng. J. Blamey DSM., Sub Lt Annear RNVR, Lt. P. Minchener (1st Lt.)., Sub Lt. E. Harding RNR (Navigator)

L to R: Sub Lt. G. McAlpine, A/B A. Morrison, L/Sto. Andy Grubb DSM., A/B G. Anderson, L/Tel. H. Campbell, L/Sto. J. Mckay, P.O. R. Walters (Coxswain)

Crew of Strongbow, who endured a fourteen hour ordeal from Japanese anti-submarine vessels.

Leading seaman (ASDICS) Len Ridge DSM. 1945

Notes From The Diary Of Lt. Com. 'Dick Raikes' DSO

.I was the 'third' hand in Clyde in 1936. After spending a week or so at Alexandria we were somewhere in the Eastern Mediterranean doing a couple of days exercising. Our PO/Tel. picked up something on the news about an Arab strike in Haifa. The Captain (H.M.C. Ionides) decided that we should perhaps investigate, and as we were only 100 miles away we surfaced and set off for Haifa. After securing alongside we got a signal to "Proceed to Haifa" with all despatch and I can remember with great pleasure we were able to reply that we were already there!

There was a huge fire burning in the town and we landed every available man to help in putting it out. The seat of this fire was a large timber yard with wood stacked 20 to 30 feet high and occupying about an acre. There was a hotel on one side, and a maternity home on the other, these girls had to be evacuated of course. The Arabs had planted a few rather amateur small bombs in the timber which added to our problems!

I think it was the next day that we had a visit from the chief of Police asking if we could help keep the railway line open to Sampah at the foot of the Sea of Galilee. The Captain asked for volunteers to drive a train and as every hand went up he re-phrased the question "Who knows how to drive a train?". Anyway we did a couple of hours shunting practice at Haifa Station and 'took over' the railway. It was narrow gauge and single track, so no signalling problems. The cruiser 'Sussex' arrived and took over. The train was derailed, and ambushed every night, so we built a truck to run just ahead of the train (see illustration) which if derailed could be put back on the lines more easily than a steam engine.

Though 'Sussex' was in command of the train, I did several trips with Lt. Com. George Duncan of that ship and it became a sort of glorified game of cowboys and indians. The Arabs were using old Banson rifles dating from W.W.1 and using bombs that Lawrence had taught them how to make in 1918.

It was all heady stuff in those days. After about six weeks the whole of the 1st Division (army) from Aldershot arrived to relieve us (HMS Sussex and submarines Clyde and Severn) so in fact we'd done quite a good job. I can't recall who actually made the truck but I'm sure the ERA's of both Clyde and Severn were involved in the manufacture and design.

Clyde and Severn's Armoured Rail Car

What I do remember is that when riding in the truck ahead of the train on a dark night... and knowing that we were sure to be ambushed at some point between Beisan and the River Jordan... we were not wholly confident of the so-called armour plating!

The track from Beisan to the Jordan meant a drop of about 4000 feet in a few miles, so the line twisted and turned and necessitated a maximum speed of about 10 m.p.h., conditions ideal for ambushing.

It was a very interesting period, and very exhausting as we were also carrying out nightly patrols trying to intercept the boats bringing illegal immigrants into Palestine.

Lt. Com. Raikes was the skipper of the submarine 'Tribune' and the wartime Commanding Officer of Seawolf and Tuna. He was in command of Tuna when she was the submarine used in the 'Cockleshell Heroes' raid.

The photographs are from the family of CPO Sam Perrin who was a telegraphist on Clyde.

"The gentleman must learn to haul with the mariners"
Sir Francis Drake

'Dick' Raikes third hand of Clyde 1936

Clyde - Malta 1930's

Commander Edward Loly & 'Dick' Raikes

Pre WWII photograph of H M Submarine Clyde and Crew

Springer, Scorcher & Sportsman

H.M. Submarine Sportsman was one of several 'S' class boats which comprised Reserve Group 'P' at the end of WWII. As an Hostilities Only rating who had signed on for an extra three years service I was with a number of colleagues who were in the same boat(s). The Korean War had kept us in past our expired time and this is why I believe many of us were in this reserve group awaiting release.
The reserve group submarines were kept in good working order by ourselves, taking each boat in turn to sea for exercises with anti-submarine craft. Springer, Scorcher, Seneschal & Sportsman were I believe R.G.P. with one crew (us) for the trot of boats.
I recall French submariners being sent to us for instructions on how to operate 'S' class boats. They were under the command of Lt. Com. Curot a charming Frenchman. Sportsman was being loaned to the French navy for an undetermined period.
On the 25th September 1952 we read in the newspaper that Sportsman (renamed Sibylle) had been lost with all hands (47) in 2600 feet of water off Cap Camarat near St. Tropez. A sad end to a most successful wartime submarine, ironically the Mediterranean was the scene of many of her triumphs.
Like Affray no one knows how the accident occurred, the debris which surfaced indicated that the submarine had been crushed to pieces at that depth (designed for 350 feet) later experiments saw the 'S' class hull collapse at a depth of around 550 feet. KTN-B.

Blockhouse 1940's 'Sandy' & Keith 'Ben' Nethercoate-Bryant

U 1105 (Black Panther)

In May 1945 the German 'Government' sent out orders to all U-boats at sea to sail to the nearest allied post and surrender. One of these boats was U 1105 which surrendered at sea to a Shackleton bomber and which event was recorded on film.

Eventually and manned by a British crew, the boat arrived in the Clyde and I was drafted to her from spare crew on HMS Forth.

Before this, I had been a 'sparks' on a British V class boat S/M Unruly and it was an exciting prospect to be a crew member of a German 'U' if only for a short time.

At this particular period, the British and Americans were very concerned about the likely future actions and knowledge to be gained by the Russians who were also in possession of captured or surrendered U-boats. It was known that Germany had developed and fitted the Schnorcel to a number of their boats U 1105 being one of them. In addition they had carried out extensive research into other areas of submarine development including fuelling systems.

With this in mind, there was an urgent need to know all that could be learned about U-boats and Allied Investigative Teams were therefore put aboard some of the surrendered boats to obtain information as quickly as possible. With their British crews the boats were sent out on sea exercises so that this factual information could be obtained under operational conditions.

Many of our exercises involved the use of the schnorcel and, generally speaking, whilst this device was fitted to enable U-boats to remain at sea for long periods of time provided they could be refuelled from the so-called 'Milch Cows' (large supply submarines), they were pretty unpleasant to the comfort of crews when in use, often causing very painful ears and discomfort to eyes.

This situation arose due to a vacuum created in the boat when the sea washed over the schnorcel head and an automatic valve shut off the head to prevent water entering the schnorcel - this also effectively shut off the air being drawn through the device which, of course, was its purpose in the first place.

In operational conditions, the schnorcel, normally lying flat on the casing, would be raised so that the head protruded just above the surface. One diesel could then be run from the air supply drawn in and so put a

charge on the batteries without the need to surface as was normally the case. One disadvantage was that the head of the schnorcel left a more distinctive wash which could be more easily detected.
Having experienced the effect of the vacuum which, apart from being hard on the ears, tended to lift you on your toes. I can imagine the long term impact this could have had on German crews when subject to the condition over long periods of time.
German submariners, like American bomber crews, enjoyed creating insignias for their boats and U 1105 was no exception. The site for these, usually well painted, insignia was the conning tower and I recollect my astonishment at the painting of a black panther draped across a globe of the world on the side of the conning tower of U 1105. I seem to recall that the boat alongside also had a painting of some sort but of that, I cannot now be sure.
'Black Panther' as the boat was named, was given this title because of the black rubber coating which completely covered the hull as a protection against asdic impulses. As far as I know, names for German U-boats were uncommon and I think U 1105 was unique both in the rubber coating and the name.
She was a much larger boat than 'Unruly' with a wide, wooden surfaced casing, grooved overall and with plenty of room for movement. Aft of the bridge, she was armed with four 20mm guns and below this a 37mm anti-aircraft gun. These armaments were fitted to some boats later in the war to give them added protection against attacks by Allied aircraft. As it happened, this in itself did not give them the protection they sought and their losses continued to increase.
Internally, the immediate noticeable difference was that the watertight doors between compartments were circular rather than the standard shape of British boats. This, I understand, was to give added strength to the boat. I was not aware of any brass or other polished metal and remember having the impression that the metal work was rather roughly finished. However, I had no opportunity to examine the engine or motor rooms so there may have been areas in the boat where this was not the case.
Everything was, of course, written in German which, in itself gave a feeling of being on foreign ground. This did not, however, constitute a problem as, basically, one diesel-electric boat is the same as another - it goes without saying that it could not have been otherwise with a British crew aboard!

Strangely enough, I was never employed as a 'Sparker' on U 1105. My main duties being to man the telegraphs and valve wheels in the control room. These valve wheels had to be cranked open and shut as directed. Our exercises were routine as far as crewing was concerned and I can only presume that the Investigative teams succeeded in obtaining the information they sought. For my own part, when these trials ended, I was returned to 'Forth' and redrafted to an 'S' boat. It was nevertheless a very interesting experience although after 48 years, memory is reducing detail to a fairly sketchy level.

U 1105 was a Type V11C submarine displacing 769 tons surfaced and 871 tons submerged. She was some 220 feet long by 20 feet beam and with a draught of just under 16 feet; 2800 h.p. surfaced 750 submerged. The boat was capable of travelling 6000 nautical miles at a speed of about 12 knots and had a fuel capacity a little in excess of 110 tons. Her safety limit dived was 440 feet.

Most of the surrendered U-boats were scuttled or otherwise sunk in 'Operation Deadlight' and details of that operation are well documented. U 1105 did not suffer that fate with nine other boats was taken to America in 1946. The British and Russians also retained 10 boats each. I have not been able to ascertain whether the unique 'Black Panther' was preserved or broken up by the Americans.

A postscript to this event was an approach to me from the U-boat Archives in Cuxhaven who are endeavouring to record the names of all British crew members who served on U 1105 and who have, since then, maintained contact with our branch of SOCA.

Telegraphist Colin (Len) Hunt Gatwick SOCA

'A web footer' A description acquired by flying boat types in the RAF. John Cruikshank V.C. (centre of group) standing on the deck of U-1105, amid flotilla of surrendered U-boats

L to R: H. M. S/M. Tuna, ‘Black Panther’, White Puma

My Early Submarine Memories

'Volunteers wanted for submarines' was my first encounter at Chatham, and after a lot of banter from the 'sign your death warrant here', P.O. who I'm sure was 'bomb happy' found myself next day at Blockhouse, blimmy! I thought must be urgent? After the D.S.E.A. course and meeting several more submarine entrants, one was a mad Irishman dominating the Stokers mess deck, I was to meet him later 'doing the rounds'. First day at sea for me was on the L23 or was it the L27 whilst schooling at H.M.S. Elfin at Blyth, then on to that great old coal burner H.M.S. Cyclops! My first proper draft was to P 511 an American (R3 1915) boat which had arrived from the U.S.A in 1941. Soon became acquainted with the lads, the majority were HO's volunteers. What a great bunch they were, the skipper was Lt. Watson who was most helpful in instruction. 'Sprog' stokers at the helm and on the hydroplanes, all was a new adventure to this lively lot. Doing the rounds... deep dives in Loch Long, Scapa, Tobermoray where we held our 'Uckers' championship (under the clock)... Dunoon... Campbeltown... where a churn of Ideal Milk was purloined, trying to get it back to the boat... Stoker Regan falling into the 'oggin' while eating his fish and chips in the blackout, and then whilst trying to get into a 'DO' by the Commando forces I came across that mad Irishman (what was his name?) having a right old punch up with them. He was off one of the H-boats alongside us, so in joined several boat's crews and a good time was had by all! Yes Campbeltown was always 'lively', what with Jan Pearce taking on half the crew of a destroyer, Billy Brown doing his 'noble art' turn, yes it was extremely lively at Campbeltown.

Getting used to life on board a submarine was taken very well with our young lot. Surviving an involuntary ramming which snapped off the periscopes we returned to Rothsey alongside Cyclops. The lads were quite thrilled to get a run ashore there, as the Ivy Benson ladies band was performing at the local. Being duty watch that night I was assisting the ERA. working on a valve in one of the ballast tanks. The ERA. who was a weighty lad squeezed through the manhole and I was passing down the tools, after about five minutes there was a clanking of tools sliding down to the bottom of the tank with the 'tiffy' following. "Are you all right?" I shouted, then with no reply sent for the 'jimmy' who was duty officer, "Alright lets get him out" he ordered, so squeezing down into the tank I found him wedged at the bottom out to the world.

After getting a rope down we managed to get him tied up, passing the other end to the jimmy telling him to pull while I tried to heave from underneath. After a lot of struggling and groaning, managed to get him up in the opening... now have you ever tried to get a flaked out chunky tiffy through a manhole? After a lot of manoeuvring, arm first then his head and shoulders, managed to get him out eventually stretched out to the world. Although knackered myself, and I don' t think the jimmy had worked so hard in his life, and seeing the tiffy in this state of repose I shouted out sharply "Up spirits" and he came round instantly, but I think I needed that more than him. Later the boys returned from their shore leave all merry and bright and recounting their experiences ashore, apparently half the crew of submarines alongside had been 'tapping up' the Ivy Benson band although not very successful. Anyway P.O. Jordan (what a helping SPO he was, couldn't do enough for the lads) brought me fish and chips from ashore, so the evening finished nice and quietly... all creeping away to their billets and kipping it off. Time was now coming up to six months aboard the P 511, and we all knew there was more serious work to be done and gradually drifted apart to different modern boats, Northern patrols, the Med., and the Far East they went, occasionally meeting some of the old crew unexpectedly in some distant place. Unfortunately a lot put down their lives and never returned, but they will never be forgotten, aye we shall remember them, Always. Bless them all.

Arthur (Tancy) Lee Stoker 1st class
Gatwick SOCA.

Translated from the original toilet paper manuscript by the editorial committee.

Wartime Poet Inspired By Campbeltown

A wartime rescue tug captain who spent some time in Campbeltown in the early 40' s visited the Courier office last week.
Captain Colmans, of Everton in Hampshire, produced a poem from his wallet which he had been carrying with him since it was written by a young sub-lieutenant on a visit to Campbeltown in 1942.
Captain Colmans said it was read all over the world by British Military personnel during the war.
The poem was written in fun and no offence was intended. It also shows how much has changed in Campbeltown since it was written.

This bloody town' s a bloody cuss
No bloody trains no bloody bus
And no one gives a damn for us
In bloody Campbeltown

The bloody roads are bloody bad
The bloody folks are bloody mad
They' d make the brightest bloody sad
In bloody Campbeltown

The bloody flicks are bloody old
The bloody seats are bloody cold
You can' t get in for bloody gold
In bloody Campbeltown

All bloody clouds and bloody rain
No bloody curbs, no bloody drains
The Council' s got no bloody brains
In bloody Campbeltown

The bloody dances make you smile
The bloody band is bloody vile
It only cramps your bloody smile
In bloody Campbeltown

No bloody sport no bloody games
No bloody fun no bloody dames
And girls don't give their proper names
In bloody Campbeltown

Everything' s so bloody dear
A bloody bob for bloody beer
And is it good? No bloody fear
In bloody Campbeltown

Best bloody place is bloody bed
With bloody ice upon your head
You might as well be bloody dead
In bloody Campbeltown

Circa 1942

The First Commission Of H.M.S. Sibyl

She was built at Birkenhead by Cammel Lairds and when completed left on 12th August 1942 for the Clyde. We arrived at Holy Loch where we tied up alongside the depot ship H.M.S. Forth. For the next four weeks we carried out all the necessary trials and working up practices.
On the 13th September, we left the Forth for our first shake-down patrol in the North Sea off the coast of Norway where it was hoped to find U-boats leaving and returning from patrol. This proved uneventful and we returned to Holy Loch on 26th September.
After 72 hours leave each watch we left Holy Loch on passage to Gibraltar in company with two other submarines, H.M.S. Splendid and H.M.S. unique on 31st October. This proved a bit more eventful. On the 9th a U-boat was sighted too near to make a torpedo attack so an attempt to ram was made but the U-boat dived and we ran over the top of her. On the 10th we were in position off Ferrol to intercept a blockade runner that was due to leave. Just after 2130 hours she was sighted and we made a surface attack on her. This proved a bit hair-raising as two of our torpedoes started circling and we had to make a hurried dive which was just as well as one of them passed across the top of us. Needless to say, the blockade runner made a run for it and managed to avoid the other two submarines that were with us.
On 12th October, we left the patrol area for Gibraltar where we arrived on the 15th October and tied up alongside H.M.S. Maidstone. Unfortunately the Unique never made it. On the 15th November we left Gibraltar for a patrol area off Toulon arriving there on the 5th. This was with company of other submarines, to keep an eye on the French Fleet in case it put to sea to interfere with the invasion of North Africa which was due to take place.
Within a few days on the 8th, we were ordered to a beach off Cap D'Antibes to pick up a party of General Giraud's staff. On arriving there we went within three hundred yards of the shore and then about 022 hours a small boat was seen coming towards us. The skipper Lieut. Turner asked for the password and was surprised to hear a womans voice answer "They seek him here they seek him there, those Frenchies seek him everywhere. Is he in heaven, is he in hell? that damned elusive Pimpernel." She proved to be an Englishwoman married to a French Officer who had been picked up the day before with General Giraud by

H.M.S. Seraph and was now on his way to Gibraltar.
In all, we picked up six men and one woman, two men and another woman had been arrested a few hours earlier by the French police.
We left straight away for Algiers arriving there on the 11th where we disembarked our honoured passengers. On the 12th we left Algiers with a small convoy of our M/V's with four escorts. Two of the M/V's were sunk before reaching Gibraltar, we again trying to ram a U-boat which also dived too soon.
We arrived back at Gibraltar on the 14th November for our next patrol - the fourth. We left Gibraltar on the 22nd November for the Gulf of Tunis arriving there on the 28th. On the 22nd December, we were warned that "Force Q" from Malta were in the area and were told to keep out of the way and watch for any ships trying to escape from the convoy that were going to attack. This they did and the look-outs on the bridge had a very good view of the convoy being completely wiped out. Only a couple of destroyers managed to escape in the dark.
We were then ordered to a new patrol area in the Gulf of Naples. On the 5th December, we intercepted a convoy consisting of two 5,000 ton M/V's escorted by three destroyers. Torpedoes were fired and three hits out of four were made sinking both of the M/V's. Sixty two depth charges were dropped in their counter-attack but none too close, this being our first sound of enemy reprisals.
We left our patrol area on the 10th December arriving in Algiers on the 14th. The Maidstone and the 8th Submarine Flotilla having left Gibraltar for Algiers thus cutting the time in half for a boat getting to and from its patrol area.
Our next two patrols in the Naples area proved unfruitful and it was not until our April patrol that we saw further activity. On the 2nd April we left Algiers for the North of Sicily where we arrived without incident. On the 11th while surfaced charging our batteries, we had to make a hurried crash dive to avoid a destroyer making straight for us and passed right over the top of us, but carried on its way as if not knowing we were there. On 11th we sighted a convoy of three medium sized M/V's escorted by six destroyers and aircraft. Four torpedoes were fired and two were heard to hit on the nearest M/V which was known later to have been sunk. We went deep but still suffered a close depth-charge attack, forcing us down even further to about four hundred feet.
This attack did not last long and we thought we had got away with it but

early in the afternoon, two destroyers with the help of aircraft, found us again and gave us another good going over dropping another 75 depth charges making 95 in all that day before breaking off the attack just after 1500 hours.
On the 13th April, we sighted another M/V escorted by two destroyers but too far away to make an attack. Shortly after this, we left our patrol area for Algiers arriving back there on the 20th April. We left Algiers again on 3rd may for a patrol off the coast of Sardinia. No targets were sighted and we arrived back in Algiers on the 19th May.
On 1st June, we left again, this time for the coast of Corsica to carry out a special operation dropping off stores and personnel and picking up agents for the return journey, arriving back in Algiers on the 16th June.
On 28th June, we were at sea again with several other submarines to cover landings about to be made on Sicily. Our area was off the North of Corsica to intercept the Italian Fleet if they should put to sea from ports in Northern Italy to interfere with these landings.
Nothing transpired from this but on the 5th July, we torpedoed and sank an M/V being escorted by an A.M.C. On the 6th we were attacked by torpedo and depth charges by an E-boat. No damage being inflicted upon us. We arrived back in Algiers on the 22nd after the disappointment of seeing targets passing out of our range.
On the 17th August, we left again to carry out another special operation in the Gulf of Genoa, arriving there on the 20th. On this one, we had to make contact with a fishing fleet and watch out for one flying certain pennants. This was done and close watch was made on where she laid her fishing nets. Apparently they were only allowed to fish during daylight hours so when they left just before dark, the nets were still left in position.
On surfacing just after dark we went alongside the nets of the boat we had been watching and started to haul them in, attaching cannisters of arms, ammunition and stores to them and dropping them back in again ready to be collected the next day. We then went off to charge our batteries, diving at daybreak and then watching the fishing fleet come out to pick up their nets which was duly done. This allowed us to carry on with our normal patrol routine, however no targets were seen so we left our area and arrived back in Algiers on the 31st August.
On the 18th September, we again left Algiers for the Gulf of Genoa area. On the 22nd, we made a possible hit on a 1500 ton M/V which

was not thought to have sunk and we were kept deep by depth charge attacks by the escorts. On 23rd, we did hit a 3000 ton ship which blew up and sank, this one was believed to be carrying petrol and ammunition. Then on 30th, we torpedoed and sank a large unescorted armed trawler fully loaded with German troops off the port of Bastia. Shortly afterwards, we left for Algiers arriving on the 4th October. This proved to be our last patrol from Algiers as the 8th Flotilla with the Maidstone were making ready to leave for the Far East.

With H.M.S. submarines Sportsman and Sickle we left Algiers for Beirut to join the 10th Flotilla, stopping at Malta for a few days for annual docking. Our next patrol, our 15th, was from Beirut where we left for the Aegean on 24th December which did not prove very popular with the crew. This was to carry out another special operation which was duly carried out. We then carried on with a normal patrol sinking a number of caiques being used to carry stores to German forces on some of the Greek islands. We arrived back in Beirut on the 13th January.

Our skipper, now Lieut. Commander Turner, was taken ill on our last patrol and was still on the sick list when we left on our next and last patrol from Beirut on 1st February with Lieut. Beale in command. This proved to be our worst patrol in the whole of the time we had spent in the Med. On the 8th February, we intercepted a convoy which included two M/V's and three escorts and were on the surface in bright moonlight when we were spotted by one of the escorts who opened fire on us forcing us to dive. Knowing just where we had dive, which was in less than 100 feet of water, they certainly gave us a going over and severely damaged us. When it was all over and we were able to surface, we found that besides external damage which was extensive, we could not use the port engine as it had been shaken off its seating. A signal was sent to Beirut requesting a recall and we were ordered to make for Malta where we arrived on the 17th February. We then spent five weeks in Malta dockyard repairing the damage and replacing the port engine on its seating. After the repairs, we did one more short patrol off the coast of Yugoslavia where an Army Captain and a Marine Sergeant we were carrying had to deliver a wireless transmitter to a group of Partisans. We dropped them off as planned and we then had to wait for three days for their return.

When the three days were up and no sign of them we thought that something must have gone seriously wrong, so we reluctantly left for Malta.

It was not until we got back to the U.K. a few weeks later that we heard that all was well with them, they having to stay behind to show how the transmitter worked and afterwards having to make their own way back to Malta.

For this patrol, we had Lieut. Commander Turner back as skipper. On 5th April, we finally left Malta for the U.K. arriving at Holy Loch on the 19th April after doing a short anti U-boat patrol off the French coast. This commission completed by the Sibyl was the longest ever of any submarine in the Med. during the Second World War. During this time we completed in all, nineteen patrols, sank seven ships by torpedo, eight by gunfire, destroyed one enemy aircraft and carried out six special missions.

After arriving back in the U.K. we sailed the boat round to Blyth where she went in for a long overdue refit which was completed. Left for the Far East with a completely new crew to rejoin the Maidstone and her Flotilla.

Bill Britton (Snr.) L/STO.

H. M. Submarine Sibyl

Crew of H. M. S/M. Sibyl with Bill Britton Snr. in overalls under gun.

The Englishman 'Ticknell'
Secret Service Agent

Sibyl crew reunion at Fort Blockhouse with Jolly Roger
Bill Britton Snr. third from right.

A B.N.L.O. In Dutch And French Submarines

In November 1942 I volunteered to serve in the Royal Navy. I had been a medical student and quite enjoying my life in war time London. The fact that many of my friends were serving and had been taken prisoner or killed worried my conscience.

I went to H.M.S. Royal Arthur in the very cold winter of 1942/43. I spent nine very instructive and enjoyable months on the lower deck till I became a C.W. candidate and later commisioned, Acting Sub-Lieutenant Ex.Sp. R.N.V.R. in December 1943. I volunteered for X-craft and was sent to H.M.S. Dolphin for forward routing to H.M.S. Varbel on the west coast of Scotland. Very early on in the course they found that my eye sight was no up to standard, certainly not up to watch keeping. The only way that I could serve in S/Ms was as a British Naval Liaison Officer. I was drafted to H.M.S. Ambrose (S 9) in Dundee. One of only three duty free shore establishments. Blyth and Lerwick being the others.

All allied submarines and surface ships working with the R.N. carried a small liaison party. In S/Ms it consisted of an officer, telegraphist and signalman. S 9 was the home base for all allied S/Ms other than U.S. Navy. It was an extremely happy place, an amazing blending of Dutch, French, Polish, Norwegian and British. The crews had left their home country some three to four years before and were bravely going on patrol in their own home waters. The Norwegians especially. French boats on patrol around their country's coast line and in the Mediterranean and likewise the Dutch in the Med. and the Far East.

After a short general course on Submarines including Codes and Cyphers I was very lucky to be drafted to H.Neth.M. S/M O 21. She had just returned to Dundee from a very successsful commission in the Far East. My liaison party consisted of two exceptional ratings. P.O.Tel W. J. Greaves and Ldg, Sig 'Andy' Hardy R.C.N.V.R. O 21 had been towed over from Holland in 1940 without her batteries. Up to when I joined her she had had a most successful productive war. She was the first Dutch S/M to sink a U-boat in W.W.2. This she did off the coast of Spain in the western Med... Lt, Cdr J. F. Van Dulm her then C.O. sank U 95 taking her C.O. captive. Van Dulm and the German C.O. became great friends after the war. When I joined O.21 Lt T. J. Krossen had just become C.O. he having previously been the number one. She was a

very happy boat but in urgent need of a big refit.
We sailed for H.M.S. Forth in the Holy Loch and then on a passage patrol to the States for the refit.
The duty of the liaison party was to assist the C.O. in all departments when in a British port; to organise the recognition signals, cyphers and codes. All S.Bs. (secret books) were under the care of the B.N.L.O. We did not speak Dutch which did not seem to matter as they all spoke very good English. One or two of the crew had married British girls.
We had a very rough crossing of the North Atlantic. O 21 lost quite a large section of her fore-casing. We were supposed to have an escort meet us off the coast of Newfoundland but they were unable to find us so we made St. Johns on our own. We then went down the East Coast via Halifax, New London, New York to Philadelphia. I had sent Andy Hardy my Canadian Signalman home on leave from Halifax. This was his first home leave for several years.
We arrived at the Navy Yard, Philadelphia on the 29th May having left Holy Loch on the 6th May. The Americans were very hospitable and it was lovely to see everything lit up at night, no rationing of food or petrol. There were several British ships in the Navy Yard being repaired or refitted including H.M.S. Nelson and I think two S/Ms. There was another Dutch S/M, I think O 24 and two French boats. One was the Pearl who was lost on her way back to the U.K. in July. She was part of a convoy and was very sadly sunk by a Fleet Air Arm plane from a carrier in the convoy. It was a terrible disaster which should never have happened.
Le Glorieux the other French boat completed her big refit in early July and I was asked to take over her liaison party. She had not had a liaison party before having not worked with the British. My two ratings Greaves and Hardy volunteered to join me which was very pleasing. Le Glorieux was a large boat of over 300 ft and very steady on the surface. She was one of five boats to escape from Toulon on the 27th Nov. 1942 when the French scuttled their fleet.
We left Philadelphia on July 7th for New London via New York, Staten Island. At New London we did our working up and then left for Casablanca with a U.S. Navy PCE. We were near Bermuda when we had trouble with our diesels. The only major part that the Navy Yard had replaced was the cooling system and it had broken down. We had to go into Bermuda where we spent four very pleasant weeks. We were at

the U.S. Navy base not the British Dock Yard. I did my best ever bit of liaison work whilst there.

I knew that there had been three or four French Destroyers working out of Bermuda in the very early months of the war. Where the French Navy is there is wine. I found three very large casks of red wine in a store in the old Dock Yard. I was very popular. we arrived at Casablanca on Sept 7th. 1944. Whilst there Le Glorieux changed her captain. I got on with the new C.O. much better than the previous one. In fact he became a good friend. After three weeks we set off to Oran which was to be our base for the next year. At Oran we lived ashore. At times there might be two or three other French S/Ms at the S/M base with liaison parties. We had quite a good life, living in a pleasant villa on the edge of the city over looking the harbour with a small weekend villa eastward along the coast at Kristel. We spent most of the time 'ping running' for ships entering the Med. on their way to the Far East. Soon after arriving in North Africa I went to Algiers to pay my respects to 'the powers that be'. I called on the C in C Western Med. He was extremely kind and interested in my job. He was quite adamant that I would find my job very much easier if I was a full Lieutenant so I went back to Oran with two rings. This set a precedent and most B.N.L.O.s in the Med. got made up to Lieutenant. I had been a sub for only eight months!

We went to Toulon at the time of the landings in the South of France. They had thought that the retreating Germans would have destroyed the power stations and we would be able to give electricity to part of the city. This they had not done but we were able to spend two most enjoyable months in Le Glorieux's old home port. Back to Oran 'ping running'.

In early May we were off to Gibraltar when the war in Europe ended. We sent a signal to N.O.I.C. Gib stating that we had run out of bread requesting permission to enter harbour. This was granted and when we tied up there was a local bakers van on the quay but it did not contain any bread! The French and my two rating celebrated in a VERY BIG WAY which was resulted in the boat being asked to move on so the next day we left for Casablanca, to have our torpedoes serviced.

In August my P.O.Tel went back to U.K., and the Canadian signalman took passage on a cargo ship back to Canada. I went to Algiers and took passage (most uncomfortable) on a L.C.Q. to Malta and became spare crew at Medway 2 S.10. Quite a place with lots of recent history of

1944 A few moments of relaxation.
Outside the Dover Castle (off Harley Street) Dr. Douglas Sinclair right of picture.

great bravery. I was there for very liquid celebration of V. J. Day.
I was not keen to go home as I knew I would have to restart my medical studies.
I joined the French Light Cruiser Le Fantasque on the 28th August and spent a most enjoyable year in the Far East, working out of Saigon. I returned home in September 1946 and resumed my medical career at The London Hospital in October. I qualified in 1952 and spent my medical life very happily in general practice.
Dr. Douglas Sinclair
24th January 1994.

Crew's Messing Arrangements Free French Submarine Casabianca

The Egg In The Oyster

By 'Choppa' (John H. Capes)

Ventilation louvres on the messdeck deflected warm puffs of air on to the sweating backs of myself, 'Choppa' and my chum, 'Scouse'. After a conflab between us we could rustle up $100 (Hong Kong) = £6 (then 16 to the £). Enough for a good night out. In the intense activity of the last few days, war having recently been declared, our departure from this excellent submarine base obviously certain and imminent.
We got the last launch to the jetty steps, Hong Kong side. On approaching the Fleet Club came across the inevitable wave of girls from the age of ten upwards, screaming "Me first time piece" this suggesting they were virgins that night. Having fought them off we emerged into the entrance of the Fleet Club, which provided excellent pints of draught 'Youngers'. We proceeded to Loo Kwoc for a couple of noggins in the sea food bar to look over the talent. Got the eye from a couple of White Russians, off-white cammels. Much too good looking to be true. Especially in the dock area of Wanchai. Scouse was raring to 'shackle up'. Cooled him off with the thought of a certain 'China chafe'. Popped out of the side entrance, extricated ourselves from the wave of struggling humanity persistent in their entreaties. Incidentally fannies approached the conception of bill poster buckets, even in those of such tender years.
We were lucky, a tram approached, and slows for us to make a jump. This is not what any ordinary person would recognise as a tram, being a kind of double-decker framework in the last possible state of desperation and dilapidation perched on two pairs of bogey wheels, groaning and screaming in protest as worn out wheels and track provide motive power. No glass windows of any kind are allowed. Will not blow over in normal typhoons. Upper deck having a horrifying sway and lurch in all conditions and weathers. We dropped off at the dockyard canteen, a more central district out of the slums.
Tombola is in full swing. Packed humanity tiered up the walls, a tense, highly perspiring mob (I term the hungry thousand). After four games, hoarse anguished whisper in my lughole "sweating"! Seconds later loud shout "Stop errr", any winnings always splitters. Half in the kitty.

Myself having the most experience and years always keep the kitty, now augmented by $64 (H.K.). In any Eastern grot, on the winning side motto is 'Instant Scapa'. Walked down to the ferry jetty. Caught the Kowloon harbour ferry boat. Similar in outline to a Mississippi River steamboat only negative wheel paddle.
Kowloon is the mainland side of Hong Kong harbour. Chinese borders being only 10 to 15 miles away. Hong Kong being in actual fact a small island with a large mountain peak in the centre. Most thickly populated in the world. Kowloon is more Yankeefied and more exotic generally. Find ourselves in the Bar B.Q. Owned by two retired U.S.N. old sweats (Heard years later were stupid enough to get caught in Jap invasion, what you would term extremely hard Gorgonzola. It goes to show my exact sentiments, however clever or crafty the outlook, stupidity clears the whole shebang).
Bar B.Q. caters for superior EWO draught and bottled, nearest equivalent I know to modern Harp Lager. The speciality in this glittering sin palace being 'Panthers Piss', a genuine North Chinese bottled beer from Macao. Was one of the few rice fermented brews I came across in my China travels, a close second to an instant explosive mixture SAM-SUI, chinese rice fermented whisky.
Myself and Scouse having sampled every form of entertainment, even to Shanghai and Mukden were in naval parlance, 'Ballroom centipedes', good dancers (originally through boredom). Dreamland Land next door to the Bar B.Q. was a small dance hall. The attraction was exotic camels in cheongsam ball gowns, 10 dances for one dollar. As an introduction to possible further interesting athletics, Scouse was wrapped round his favourite Ah-Sin very statuesque and thoroughly warmed up now, about midnight.
Myself sneaked back for further liquid refreshment and a quick look in at the Savoy Ballroom, Suzy was in great form, didn't barge in.
About an hour later got Scouse out of Dreamland. Rickshaw each to Kowloon ferry. On reaching Hong Kong side thought oysters would settle our liquor more comfortably. Close by was Jimmy's Kitchen, renowned sea food for all appetites, oysters at $10 dozen. Had a couple each. Again rickshaws to China Fleet club and comfortable doss till 7 a.m. , tea and 7.30 liberty boat aboard.
Two weeks later submarine was at sea, likely shadowing some vessel up the coast. Steady thunderous roar from diesels in main engine room.

Steady slight roll and enjoyably cool for a change. Week goes by. Supper is up 10 p.m. In these early halcyon days we had a civilian Chinese mess steward, named chug. Had been aboard a year, a real jewel, he got 10 dollars a month from each of the fourteen of us, in full charge of all rations, which he augmented from family shoreside. We were all curry fiends. The national Chop Suey in a hundred and one gorgeous ways. Relieved Scouse for supper on engine centre platform. 360 revs., steady bellow from exhaust going to cooling drenchers. 20 minutes later relieved and back in the messdeck. Chug was washing up the messtraps (crockery), said Scouse take plenty chow, hungry, not belong much chow seaside, poor appetite. Week went by, steady passage routine. Two night diving station routines. Relieve Scouse again for supper. Now always abnormally hungry. Off watch dead on his bunk, not a word out of him. Apparently severely off colour.

Next night in the mess was curled up in his bunk with severe stomach pains. Chug did his middle watch. Scouse still tucking away large quantities of food and having the most severe spasms. Mumbled to me thought he was in the spud line. Became semi-conscious, was carried to a bunk in the passageway forward to the petty officers quarters. Coxswain acts as sick berth attendant and thus keeps a close observation. Next day Scouse was groaning and completely out. All next week saw himdaily and nightly. Coxswain mentioned his stomach was expanding/" daily. Now, completely unconscious and groaning, big jabs of morphine. Day later returned to dockyard No. 2 jetty. Scouse rapidly tied in collapsible stretcher and swung on to the jetty by large crane. Quickly changed into clean tropical gear. On jetty from HMS Tamar was portable trolley with four bike wheels, motive power being four barefoot Chinese seamen, looked like refugees from Snow White's seven dwarves.

Scouse quickly settled on it, smartly sped away with me in close pursuit to dockyard sick quarters. Eternal waiting, missed dinner aboard, he had been moved from there. Returned to find very excited R.N. X-Ray assistant. Showed me large stomach photo. Incredible to relate was clear faint outline of oblong vertical object with small parrots beak in the top half about the size of a medium grapefruit. Quick conference to account for this incredible thing. Told doctor we were together and had oysters in Jimmy's Kitchen about six weeks previously. Immediate caesarian operation was highly successful.

Three nights later packed Scouse's kit and took it to him at Tamar. Being of a hardy nature quickly recovering and full of beans.
Saw octopus in sealed pickle jar. His most prized possession, and the X-ray pictures. We were off for good that night, he was left behind to follow in OD. Never saw him again. Was lost at sea in 1940. Evidence never reached Royal College of Surgeons. Would have set them up all right.

Beast Born of Man Sworn to be the truth by John H. Capes.

(If this story is true the submarine was the Olympus KTN-B)

Copied from his original MSS. for Submarine Memories.

OLYMPUS
Submarine of "Egg in the Oyster"

Surrender Of U-2326 At Dundee.
Dundee Telegraph Evening Of 14th May 1945

A German U-Boat, U-2326 surendered at Dundee harbour today at 9.30 am. The crew only learned yesterday that Germany had capitulated, as their wireless was out of order. This is one of Germany's latest type of submarine 250 tons and 100 feet long (Type XXIII, Ed.). She was met at the bar of the Tay by a Royal Navy motor launch, who handed her over to the fishing smack 'Taefing' ? The U-Boat approached the eastern end of King George Wharf, flying the insignia of surrender, and her German naval insignia. Dockers and shipworkers downed tools and crowded into wagons to see, many even climbed cranes.

Safely alongside, an R.N. P.O. pulled down the German flag, and the German captain, and a number of officers in the conning tower stood to attention and gave a military salute, the flag of surrender was ripped off, and the white ensign hoisted. First ashore were two young officers then two ratings, the second of whom clapped his hands as he stepped onto the quay. On shore the crew of fifteen, wearing green-grey uniforms, blue forage caps and overalls. They were lined up to be searched. Knives and pipes were their only possesions. Two of the crew had the Iron Cross. They were unshaven but looked sturdy and well fed. The watching crowd had swelled to over a thousand and were kept in check by a Norwegian with a fixed bayonet.

A Dutch naval rating acted as interpreter, and he told the senior officer that the boat would be searched for explosives (small arms and ammo. Tommy guns and a scuttling charge were found).

The crew stood on the jetty for over an hour, and they were greatly interested in a 'Barracuda' bomber and two 'Mosquitos' flying around the harbour. The German commander and the engineer officer who had accompanied the search officers appeared in the conning tower carrying maps and charts, talking to a naval officer. Captain W. F. Keay took the commander, who saluted as he stepped ashore, in a car, along with another German officer for interrogation. The crew were dismissed by their officer, and returned to their boat under escort. She had six days stores in her. She is to remain in the Tay before joining the rest of her pack at some assembly point.

U-2326 Docking at Dundee

Crew of U-2326 (see newspaper report)

U-Boat Captain Jobst surrendering to Dutch Naval Officer

Photographs by kind permission of Dundee Telegraph

Report On The Surrender Of U-2326

After the surrender of Germany on the 8th May 1945, the German high command were instructed to issue orders to U-Boats still at sea to surrender. Their orders were to surface, remain surfaced, signal U-Boat number and position. Fly a black flag by day and illuminate their navigation lights by night. Make for ports designated by the Allies, by set routes. Jettison all ammunition, make torpedoes safe by removing the firing pistols and render any mines safe.

Captain Jobst of U-2326 stated that he was well out in the North Sea and only knew the positions of the minefields in the northern part of the North Sea and decided to make for Kiel. Later that day and again on the 12th May he heard the full surrender instructions and stayed on the surface flying a black flag. At 0700 on the 12th a Liberator aircraft flew over the U-Boat. Jobst signalled the aircraft giving his U-Boat number and his intention of heading for Kiel.

Again at 1200, on the 12th, another Liberator flew over the U-Boat, once again Jobst signalled his intention to make for Kiel. Two minutes later the aircraft circled the U-Boat and dropped a bomb nearby. Jobst stopped the boat and was instructed by the Liberator to steer course 270 degrees and make for Loch Eriboll. The last signal he claimed to have received from the aircraft was "See you in Dundee" ... This he took to mean make for Dundee. Whilst on passage Jobst made contact with HMS Vivien and was told to proceed for Edinburgh. By the 14th U-2326 had reached the Bell Rock, there Jobst waited for further instructions. A patrol boat soon arrived and escorted the U-Boat into Dundee.

At the end of 1944 and the early part of 1945 the British and U.S. started to draw up plans for trials of captured and surrendered U-Boats. They wanted to keep and evaluate two of every kind of submarine. U-2326 was a new boat and a smaller edition of the type XXI which were just coming into service at the end of the war.

Little details are known about this U-Boat, she was towed to France, presumably for the French Navy to inspect. She was reported lost with all hands on 5th December 1946 off Toulon*. The cause was given as a welding defect.

* Another report suggests the sub went down off the Bay of Biscay in 1947 with a French crew aboard.

His Majesty's Submarine 'Ambush'

Ambush was completed in 1947 at Vickers Yard, Barrow in Furness. On trials we went to the hundred fathom line in the Atlantic and did our deep dive to five hundred feet, she took it well. After all the other trials the boat was accepted on behalf of the Admiralty by then Lt.Cdr. G. E. Hunt DSO★ DSC who remained with us until he was made Commander. He instilled confidence and respect in everyone who served with him. A great loss to the Submarine Service when he was retired with the rank of Captain.
In 1948 under the command of Lt. A. G. Davies R.N. we were sent to the Arctic to try out the 'Snorkel' in bad weather. This was successfully carried out in March 1948. Later in the year Ambush in the company of another 'A' boat carried out trials in the Scottish Lochs of trying to fuel another boat under water. Not a great success, and as far as I know it was never tried again*. I left the Ambush in September 1948 as I had finished my time.

'Bill' Sherrington Ldg. Sig. V-pres. London SOCA - member Gatwick.

Under the Arctic Ice Bill Sherrington Centre Below

* Underwater re-fuelling was carried out in the Solent in the late 1940's, I was a Stoker 1st class serving in Reserve Group 'P'. I believe we fuelled either 'Scorcher' or 'Springer' from a 'T' class which may have been 'Tiptoe'.

KTN-B.

‘A’ Class Submarine surfacing

Ship’s company H. M. S/M Ambush
Portland November 1947

Ambush in the Arctic
"Up Spirits"

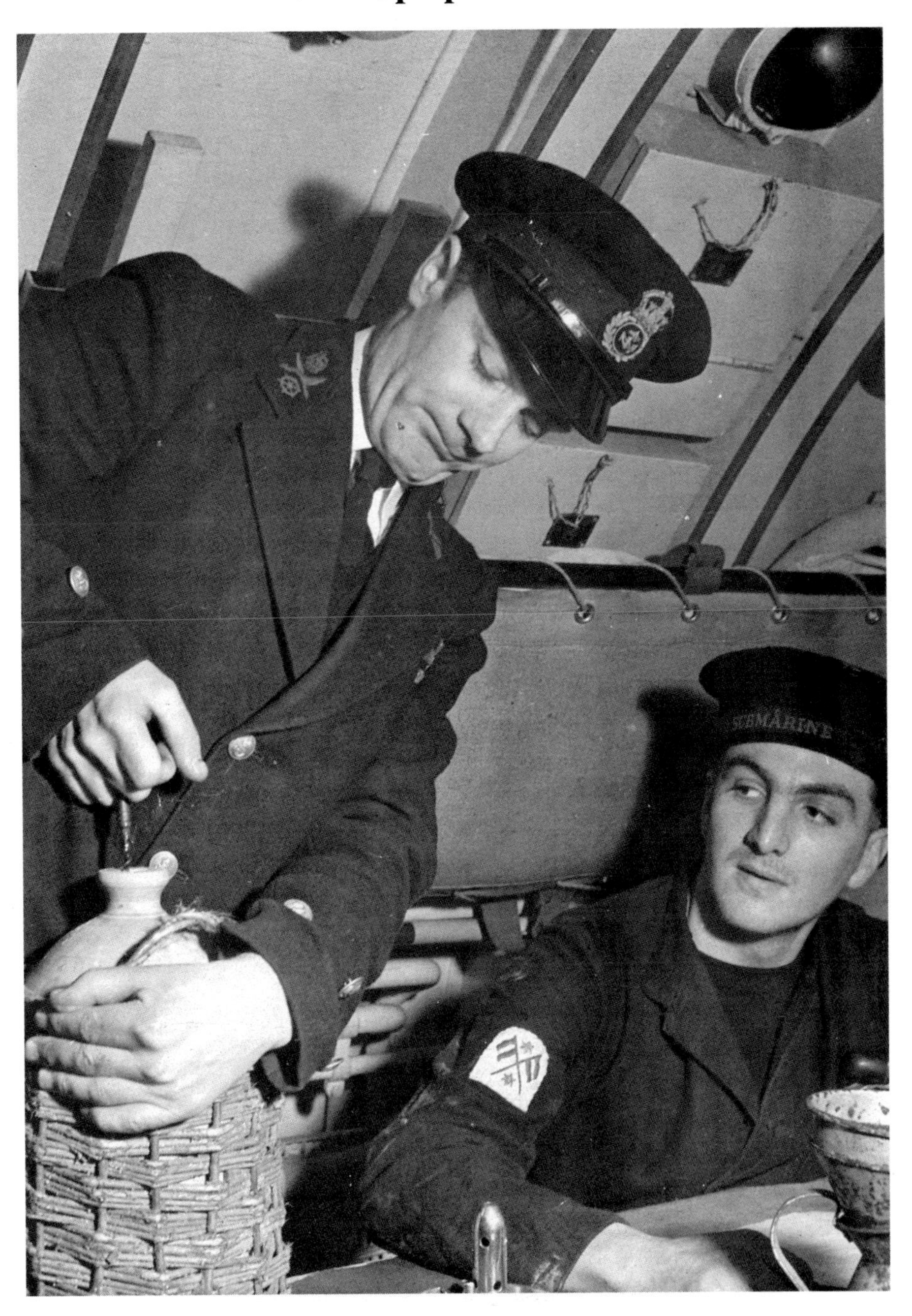

Coxswain 'Grocer' Greer. Ldg. Sig. Bill Sherrington

H.M.Submarine Ambush top heavy with ice
Arctic Ocean 1948

His Majesty' s Canadian U-Boat 190

The photograph below is not of a German.submariner but Frank Dedman who served on U-190. The uniform was left aboard by one of the submarines former crew members. The boat was a type IXc/40 these were used as transports among other duties, U-190 was, with U-889, taken to Halifax and handed over to the Canadian Navy. Some of the British crew remained to instruct the Canadians on their operation.

U-889 & U-190 - Halifax, Nova Scotia 1945

The British & Canadian crew of U-190

U-1407 - HMS Meteorite

U-Boat 1407 was a type XVIIb it was an improved experimental type XVII powered by a Walter high test peroxide engine designed to propel the boat for short periods at speeds approaching 25 knots.

U-1407 was recovered from the sea off Cuxhaven where it had been scuttled on the night of the 5/6th May and brought back to the UK by the then Lt. Paul Chapman DSO. OBE. DSC★ . It was refurbished at Vickers Barrow-in-Furness with the help of Dr. Walter and some of his staff.

The boat was renamed 'Meteorite' and did a series of trials in Morecombe Bay between 1947 and 1949 achieving high speeds. It was difficult to control as there were no forward hydroplanes. I remember it had an aircraft type control which was dependant on the skill of the helmsman at speed.

Out of these trials came the British experimental submarines 'Explorer' and 'Excaliber' later because of certain incidents dubbed 'Exploder' and 'Excruciator'. Other features from these craft were adopted for our 'S' class boats several adapted for high speed ping running used the streamlined conning tower, among them SOLENT, SELENE, SATYR, SERAPH AND STATESMAN.

I was only on board for a short period to replace a stoker who fell sick but I remember a demonstration by Dr. Walter of the volatile HTP fuel.

A colleague of mine Les Enticknap reminded me of an incident after trials when tied up alongside the tender 'Woodbridge Haven'. The periscope was raised to secure a steaming light to it, and on pushing off the periscope was caught on Woodbridge Haven's anchor producing a curly periscope (a cartoon exists recording this event).

Meteorite was scrapped c.1950. KTN-B

Artemis is born

Artemis

Artemis was an 'A' class submarine built by 'Scotts' Shipbuilding and Engineering Co. Ltd. Greenock. The class were built primarily for the war in the Far East. Artemis was laid down on the 28th February 1944, the war ended in 1945 and with the diminished urgency for more submarines she was not launched until 26th August 1946. She was first commisioned on the 19th March 1947.
Artemis was 1120 tons surfaced and displaced 1620 tons submerged, she was 281 feet 9 inches long, had a beam of 22 feet 3 inches and a depth of 16 feet 9 inches. Her crew numbered c. 61. Her twin screws were driven by two sets of Diesel engines and or two electric motors, she had a range of 10,500 miles at 11 knots with a top speed of 18fi knots surfaced and 8 knots submerged. Artemis's armament was quite formidable for the time, she had 6 21" bow torpedo tubes, 4 21" stern tubes and carried 20 torpedoes, she also had a 4" deck gun, a 20mm A.A. gun and 3 machine guns. She was also able to carry up to a total of 26 mines.

Artemis after her conversion in 1958/9, in this mode she was fitted with a deck gun for a short period. In 1965 she was provided with a telescopic 'snort' mast to replace the earlier one installed c. 1950. After her streamlining in the '50s Artemis made a training film 'Voyage North' which included a diving sequence often used in television films. Two of her sister ships had more luck with their filming, one took part in the film of Neville Shute's book 'On the Beach' and another featured in the James Bond epic, 'You Only Live Twice'.

Artemis is the Greek goddess of maidenhood and the twin sister of Apollo. Artemis was identified with the Roman god Diana, and regarded as patroness of hunting and the goddess of the Moon. At Ephasus her cult was modified in accordance with the worship of the asiatic deity Ashtoreth or Astarte. She was worshipped as goddess of fertility and protectoress of sailors. As goddess of fertility Artemis was depicted by the statue of the many breasted wolf suckling Romulus and Remus. A 'hunter's' Moon and a quiver of arrows is the crest of the submarine Artemis.

'Artemis' in 1950, she was engaged in 'snort' exercises in the Solent. The photographers (below) were in an accompanying motor launch. The snort mast can be seen retracted (above) on the Port side. The fracturing of this mast in her sister submarine 'Affray' was thought to be the cause of her loss in 1951.

The periscopes and 'snort' mast of Artemis. The Isle of White is in the background (above). The snort mast showing the float valve (both photos). Poor depth keeping could lift the valve shut with the diesel engines running, which caused a vacuum in the boat. Many members will remember the discomfort to the ears when this occurred.

ARTEMIS Late 1940's

Back Row: A/B D. R. Smith, Sto. H. Walsh, Sto. J. Twist, Sto. T. Nurse, Tel. R. Stills, Sto. J. Chandler, A/B N. A. Holloway, A/B E. Mulvey, Sto. C. Thompson, Sto. A. Burfield, A/B R. Burge, A/B N. Pindar, A/B G. Anderson, A/B K. B. Martin, Sto. K. T. N-Bryant, A/B J. Berry, Sto. R. Mack.

2nd Row from back: L/Stwd. J. S. Barnfield, S.P.O. F. Gallagher, S.P.O. H. Brettle, L/Sea. C. J. Peacey, L/Sea. F. Dunn, L/Sig. D. D. Jeffs, L.E.M. A. A. Campbell, L/Sea. F. Pantling, P.O. Tel. F. Matchett, E.A. K. J. Spencer, Elec. D. R. Ewen, P.O. G. Munro, E.R.A. G. Crane, E.R.A. R. F. Rebbeck, L/Tel. G. Svenson, L/Sea. R. D. Wells.

3rd Row from back: L/Sea. D. Collins, C.P.O. (coxw.) J. (Snowey) Tumman, C.S.P.O. R. J. Phebey DSM., E.A. C. J. Walker, Mid. J. A. Matson, Lt. J. M. Jessop, Lt. (E) R. D. L. Clarke, Lt. Cdr. M. L. C. (Tubby) Crawford DSC★ , Lt. W. J. Kirkwood, Lt. G. H. F. Frere-Cook, S/Lt. I. G. Riley, CERA. A. E. Burden DSM., E.R.A. G. Traves, E.R.A. P. Dammerall, L/Tel. T. W. Stephenson.

Front Row: Cook A. Anderson, A/B J. H. Butler, Sto. R. Aram, Sto. F. Slater, E.M. P. D. Hulme, A/B G. W. Hoadley, A/B M. Dennelly, E.M. T. Pirie, E.M. P. F. Price, A/B S. Goold, Sto. S. N. Benford, Sto. G. A. Tranter, Sto. J. Bason, Sto. E. Johnson.

The photograph was taken at Old Trafford on the Manchester Ship Canal, after an exercise in Northern waters and following visits to Aalesund, Bergen and other Norwegian ports. (War in Korea was declared at this time).

Lt. Com T. Hale Artemis 1967

Escape From Artemis

The best escape system in the world went into immediate operation on July 1 1971, when the submarine H.M.S. Artemis sank alongside the jetty at H.M.S. Dolphin.

Navy News spoke about the incident to Lieut.-Cdr. Matthew Todd, Flotilla Escape and Diving Officer on the staff of Flag Officer Submarines.

Lieut.-Cdr. Todd has trained thousands of submariners in escape procedures and has himself "escaped" in exercises at sea a couple of dozen times. This is in addition to hundreds of simulated escapes.

"We could have got the men out at any time," he said, "but the Artemis was leaning over so that the escape hatch was overhung by the ballast tanks of the submarine Ocelot alongside - O.K. for an emergency escape, but better to improve the situation when there is no immediate danger.

"The three men inside the submarine were kept informed by telephone, and their families knew exactly what was going on.

"The salvage teams assembled in remarkably quick time, and it was decided to wait until they got a wire round the bow of the Artemis, perhaps giving a lift, but mainly to turn the submarine more to the upright.

"They succeeded in getting the bow from beneath the Ocelot.

"Two divers were then positioned outside the Artemis escape hatch as a further precaution to steer the escapers out of any trouble, and the three men came to the surface in 'copy book' style in the manner in which they had be trained."

Lieut.-Cdr. Todd had the highest praise for the speed of the salvage operations.

He emphasized, however, that "escape by salvage" is not the Royal Navy method, though this is a subject constantly looked at, and it will be studied again in the re-examination of escape procedures which was decided upon before the Artemis incident.

The Royal Navy's present escape methods have been developed to a standard which has been copied throughout the world.

The long night

The morning after

Reading from Left to right Satyr ships company C. September 1944

E.R.A. E. Mister, P.O. M. Gooding MID, Sto. J. Danby, Sto. J. Boyes, P.O. T.I. S. Patterson DSM.,

A/B. A. Chambers, A/B. M. Stafford, P.O. Tel. H. Budd, L. Sto. L. D. Hedges, Sto. J. Stenning MID,

A/B. W. Perett, Sto. J. Norgate, L. Sea. A. Sperring, A/B. J. Baker MID, P.O. Tel. D. MacBeath,

E.R.A. Fee DSM., A/B H. A. Chinn, Tel.W. L. Walker, Sto. P.O. M. Rowan, EM. E. Roe, L. Tel. A. Purse,

A/B H. C. Smith, L. Sto. D. Cave, A/B J. Atkinson, Sto. J. Pacey, E.R.A. C. Sothcott, Sto. L. J. Jones,

A/B J. W. Smith, E.R.A. W. Rawlence, A/b R. Nicholson, A/B J. Quinn, A/B W. Anderton, A/B R. Salt,

A/B H. Butterworth, Tel. R. Christian, P.O.Ck. E. Firth, A/B R. Thexton MID, A/B P. Freeland,

Sto.P.O. N. Clarke, L. Sto. D. Jones MID, Sto. W. Bailey, L. Sea T. Moorey, L. Sig. W. Pearce DSM.,

C.P.O. P. Suter DSM., A/B E. Turner.

Satyr Officers

Reading from left to right:
Wt. Eng. D. Worsfold, Lt. P. P. B. Bennett, Sub. Lt. Goscombe RNVR., (Skipper) Lt. T. S. Weston DSO. DSC★, Lt. W. McLaughlin MID., Sub. Lt. J. H. Douglas RNVR..

A True Yarn

Accomodation at Port Said (Southways) included dormitory with a gable roof. There was midnight leave at the time and this particular bloke always came off shore about 10 minutes to midnight, full of beer and bonhomie and singing, thereby disturbing everyone who had their heads down. There was a very dim blue (police) light in the dormitory... Well we got the co-operation of Ken Muscat, a PO Writer attached to the shore base. Like myself, he was a little fellow, with a very dapper Imperial set (have you ever heard the rumour, unconfirmed, that it is a court martial offence to make a hangman's knot? Alleged to be linked to the mutiny at Spithead). Any rate we took two hammock lashings and slung them over the cross beam just inside the door. One was a bowline on the bight, by means of which under his arms, with armpits padded, we hoisted Ken up. The other was round his neck in a hangman's knot. We timed this carefully. When we heard 'yer man' starting up the stairs, he pushes the door open and of course it fouls Ken's body suspended from behind the door. Eventually 'Noisy' gets into the dormitory, takes a few steps, returns to the swinging figure (Ken had his tongue out and head to one side) he takes his cigarette lighter, flashes it up, looks at Ken, says "About time too", staggers off and turns in!

Dickie Elliot. Gatwick SOCA.

Seated (left) Yeo. Sig. Bennetts, Seated (right) P.O.TGM. Holmes, Standing Seaman P.O. Unnamed - HMS/M Rorqual, Southways

HMS/M Unruly -(A proper naval salute)

Fresh Air And Exercise!

Under the ice cap to the North Pole, HMS/M Grampus 100 miles into the Arctic ice.

Commander R. Compton-Hall M.B.E. (the Skipper) relates that the football match took place at midday on the 22nd March 1963 during operation Skua. The recorded temperature was 22 degrees F below freezing.

H. M. Submarine Aeneas

4th Submarine Flotilla Suva 15th June 1947

Seated (L to R) - C.E.R.A. Blee W.H., Lt. D. Y. Roberts (nav.), Lt/E C.E.N. Deane, Lt. W. P. McLoughlin 1st Lieut., Lt. T. S. Weston DSO DSC★ (Capt.), "O/S. Chokker", Lt. I. H. D. Rankin Torpedo Off., C.P.O. G. Waite Cox'n., Chief Stoker J. McCallum.

Standing - P/O King N.E., E.R.A. Finney K., E.A. Probee D., E.R.A. Smith B. J., S.P.O. Harney H., P/O R.M. Elliot R. N., T.G.M. Dawson H. C., P/O Beach W. E., E.R.A Morris D., E.R.A. Hazlewood S., P/O Richardson E., L/Elec. Mate Campbell A. A.

Third Row - A.B. Nixon R., Sto I/C Gordon J., A.B. Tidley W. G., L/Stwd. Lai Sang, A.B. Roper A., Sto I/C Cavender H., Sto I/C Peacock J., L/Sig. Higgs T. H., O.B. Hibbert J., Sto I/C Hodges T., Sto Thompson J., A.B. Cooze W., L/S Yates W. W., Sto I/C Black A., A.B. Steenson R.

Back Row - L/Sto French E. N., Sto I/C Pearman N. E., Sto I/C Sullivan J., A.B. Puckett H., Tel. Almond R., L/Tel. Grimes W., Sto I/C Gofton C., A.B. Pease W., A.B. Hammond S., Sto I/C Lansdown N. G., Sto Linham R. B., Sto Farran H., L/Sto Jones L. J., A.B. Talbot W., L/S McLachlan D., L/Stwd. Loo Por.

H. M. Submarine Aeneas

Rear Admiral 'Tony' Whetstone C.B. (President National SOCA.)
Turpin's Conning Tower
"A photograph that we prepared earlier!"

'Turpin' After conversion

‘Hauling in the hoses’

S-Class boat underwater refuelling from a T-Class in the Solent c.1949.

HMS/M H.8 - Photograph from Naval airship c.1917

Photograph from Naval Airship C.2 from Mullion Naval Airship Station
showing H.11 and H.12 at 10.12 on the 9th May 1918 from an altitude of 500 feet

Frank Brown (Gatwick member) in HMS Affray's conning tower. Affray failed to surface during an exercise on the morning of the 17th April 1951. It is thought that she was lost due to the failure of the snort mast. Her Skipper was Lt. Blackburn DSC who had served under Ben Bryant on *Safari*

H.M.Submarine Token

Alec Wingrave (Chairman of London and Merton branches of SOCA)
Down the hatch HMS/M Token.

H.M.Submarine Token Portsmouth.

H. M. Submarine Tireless, Australia 1945. David Gilbertson (Gatwick Member) 7th from left top row.

Two Type XVII U-boats at Kiel

These were experimental boats with HTP engines recovered at Howaldswerk Kiel by the advancing Naval forces.

U-792 Kiel 1945

U-793

HMS/M Shakespeare (The unsinkable submarine)

Shakespeare was a 1940's class submarine, an enlarged and more powerful version of the pre-war class. The vessel was built at Vicker's Shipyard Barrow-in-Furness, and commissioned by the Royal Navy in 1941. She was 220 feet long and was driven by two 8 cylinder Admiralty diesel engines and Admiralty electric motors 1900BHP (1300 SHP), speed was 14.75 knots on the surface and 9 knots (max) submerged. Her main armament comprised seven 21" torpedo tubes, and she carried 13 torpedoes. As secondary armament she was equipped with a 3" gun, a 20mm quick firing Oerlikon, 3 Vicker's machine guns and Thompson submachine guns. Radar was subsequently installed.

In 1943 she was being refitted at Devonport, and the submarine's two 225 volt ebonite covered batteries were removed, and fresh battery containers of a significant new type were installed. An invention for the construction of "unbreakable" battery containers had been patented in 1942, and a year later were proved and adopted by the Admiralty. Each battery, weighing approximately 8 Tons and standing 4 feet high, contained 112 cells. Experience had proved that ebonite castings were liable to be cracked or fractured by near misses from aircraft bombs or depth-charges, while other vital parts of the submarine might escape damage. The new containers were made of resin-bonded layers of wood and the Shakespeare was one of the first submarines to be fitted with this device which was untested under wartime conditions.

When the submarine was ready for active service Lt. David Swanston DSC★ was appointed her commander. David Swanston was a brilliant and daring young officer who entered the Royal Navy in 1932 as a Dartmouth cadet. In 1939 he volunteered for the submarine service and thereafter served in a number of submarines in the Mediterranean.

In April 1944, I was drafted as a Leading Telegraphist to the Shakespeare as a member of his crew of 46 officers and men. After training we went out on a fortnights patrol between Scotland and Norway which proved uneventful. In the early Autumn we were posted to the Far-East and became part of the Second Submarine Flotilla under Captain J. E. Slaughter at Trincomalee.

A cool evening breeze ruffled the glassy waters of the harbour as the Shakespeare slipped her moorings from the Depot ship HMS Wolfe on the 20th December 1944. She was escorted by the Maid Marian out to

sea on what was to be a 14 day patrol along the East coast of the Anderman Islands, in the middle of the Bay of Bengal (Japanese occupied) about 1000 miles from our base.
The submarines instructions were "To attack the enemy and report any important forces sighted". At midnight we reached longitude 82 degrees East at which point the Maid Marian left us and we went alone on a relentless search for enemy shipping. The first objective was Port Blair, a seaport of the Andamans, a former Indian penal settlement. On the third day of the patrol while we were approaching Ten Degree Channel, the strip of sea between the Andamans and the Nicobar Islands. Three Japanese long range flying-boats were spotted scouting around the channel. Swanston promptly submerged and took us to a safer depth, and until he was sure we had not been detected held his course for Port Blair.
After two more days of empty skies and seas we were close to Ross Island just off the entrance to Port Blair. It was now Christmas eve and Swanston decided we would have a holiday on Christmas Day. The few available spaces were decorated with Christmas trimmings (Fairy lights on torpedoes were not considered appropriate!), and we were relieved of all but essential duties. At 0100 (while waiting for Father Christmas to deliver his presents!) and cruising at about 70ft Shakespeare jolted sharply as we struck a ridge on the Ocean bed but luckily suffered no damage.
At approximately 0800 we were lying submerged off Ross Island, when Swanston peering through the periscope sights spotted the mast and funnels of a ship 2 miles North of the Island. What appeared to be a subchaser disappeared through Nankauri Strait, between two of the islands and he decided to "hang about" in anticipation that it would return with something worthwhile. Eventually it again came into view and he saw it was signalling two food carrying sampans about 3 miles west of Neill Island. At about 1430 the sub-chaser passed us with six sampans in tow following a course of about a mile offshore for Port Blair. Although the convoy was within half a mile of us, Swanston decided to wait for bigger things, and during the night he surfaced and we patrolled off Neill Island.
On Boxing day we ventured sufficiently close to Port Blair to sight the harbour and found it was empty. At 1200, three Japanese planes flew over the Port and 30 mins later the sub-chaser passed by near Sesostris

Shoal. As the harbour offered no rewarding targets Swanston changed course to patrol the Shoal, and to cover Stewart Sound. Rain and low clouds were experienced for several days and eventually he turned back for Port Blair. At 0840 on 31st December while we were submerged at periscope depth three Japanese aircraft flew low over the water without detecting us. The next day a southbound convoy was sighted leaving Nankauri Strait. The convoy consisted of one leading ship estimated at 2000 tons and a smaller one, escorted by three vessels, one stationed 1500 yards ahead, and one 1500 yard on either beam. Escorts were weaving at 15 knots and the convoy was doing a continuous zigzag. An attack was begun at 0814, and at 0912 six torpedoes were fired at the leading ship at a range of 1500 yards. Five explosions were heard, and we considered that the ship had been sunk (later confirmed) now we could put the first bar on our Jolly Roger. Then followed a concerted counter attack and it was estimated more than nine depth-charges were dropped, all fortunately missing the target. At 1130 Swanston brought the Shakespeare to periscope depth and observed one of the escorts and three planes continuing to search, he then decided to return to the former depth.

With the Japanese now aware of our presence he decided to take cover by moving away from the port until 2nd January 1945. At 0015 the same day we received a wireless signal ordering us to look for an American Liberator aircraft which was reported to have crashed 350 miles north-east of Port Blair. At 0450 this was cancelled and we stayed on the surface and set course for the Nankauri Strait.

Most wartime submarine crews had characters whose individual profiles contributed to the efficiency and not least the relationship under sometimes almost intolerable conditions. Our first Lt. John Lutley RN was a model of efficiency and was easily approachable. Sub Lt. Andrew Morgan RNVR was a keen amateur photographer and though unauthorised was constantly in action with his ancient camera. P.O.Tel Victor George Harmer was a robust overweight pot-bellied and scruffy wireless genius. His nickname 'Guts' was a reminder of his general habit of wearing his shorts below the waistline which usually concealed his knees. Another item of unofficial 'rig of the day' was the wearing of large unlaced boots at all times. The other personality was Frederick Gibbons a short service able seaman. A true Cockney, without ambition to higher rating, he was always amusing and a source of practical jokes.

Taken During The Action

3" Guns Crew. 'Substitutes' after the Jap's had 'cleared' the original with their first shot. Second left (smoking) LT. Lutley DSC. 1st Lt. H.M.Submarine Shakespeare

In fact he epitomised the strength and experience of a true submariner.
At 0530 on 3rd January, Swanston was standing on the bridge gazing over an expanse of blue listless water when he sighted the mast and funnel of a south bound ship thought to be a Shimshu class escort and immediately gave the order for diving and as the escort was alone presumed it was carrying out an anti-submarine sweep and we remained submerged. At 0715 the mast and funnel of a south bound merchant ship was sighted, an attack was begun but the range could not be closed to less than 3500 yards. At 0750 four torpedoes, spread over one and a half lengths individually aimed were fired, all torpedoes missed. As the vessel was unescorted and no aircraft were in sight we surfaced at 0758 and approached the vessel at full speed with the guns crew closed up on the 3" gun they assessed the range of the quarry and fired their first shell.
The Japanese vessel had drawn further away before the guns crew had got the range, but it turned towards us and opened fire with a 12 pounder gun from about 5000 yards. Swanston altered course 20 degrees to Port and the Oerlikon was used to fire at the target, but after a few rounds the gun jammed. A sub-chaser creeping through the Strait and hidden by the hull of the Merchant ship was seen to be racing after us, guns firing as she coursed through the water, Swanston ordered "Clear the bridge".
As Swanston prepared to leave the bridge Shakespeare rocked violently, and water cascaded down the vessels side and the bridge was riddled with holes. A 12 pounder shell had ripped a gash approximately 10" long and 5" wide in the pressure hull, just above the water line and the sea was pouring through the gap. The deluge flooded the auxiliary machinery space which housed the gyro and main compass, and flooded the control room and engine room. The ballast pump which had been started to stem the flow, flooded and broke down, water poured over the wireless transmitter and put it out of action. I experienced an unplanned and unexpected takeoff! while at my action station in the wireless office!
The outside ventilating trunking system to the battery had been shattered, and the engine room bulkhead door had to be left open. Efforts to seal the battery compartment were made before the sea forced through and cut off the battery supply of power. We were wallowing helplessly unable to dive, and open to attack from the Japanese ships and any air-

Ken Wade & 'Guts' Harmer repairing hole in pressure hull during the action.

2nd Coxw. P.O. Ted Jones.
A few seconds after shooting down first attacking Japanese aircraft.

Wt. Eng. Hodges.
Watching attacking Japanese aircraft

craft that might be summoned to deal the final blow. After inspecting the damage Swanston accompanied by Sub-Lt. Morgan And Lt. Pearson RNVR went back to the bridge. Shakespeare was now under heavy fire from the sub-chaser, but no further damage was caused at this stage.
Standing in the control room which was flooded to knee level 'Guts' Harmer and I exchanged glances and proved that mental telepathy exists and works. Without further conversation, I said "Let's go" and we proceeded to the fore-ends grabbed blankets, hammocks and locker cushions and went up the conning tower and sighted the hole just aft of the Oerlikon gun platform. Lying on my stomach I gripped 'Guts' who had his feet in the hole endeavouring to effect a temporary repair. Four more shots from the sub-chaser were on target and one of these ricocheted on the casing blowing off Harmer's prize boots and my shirt and shorts. His feet were burned and we both appeared to have been prepared for 'Jungle warfare' but continued our efforts on plugging the hole.
Able seaman Frank Foster, the gun layer and Able Seaman R. Whitelaw had both been injured, and Lt. Lutley and Telegraphist Britton took their places on the 3" gun.
Swanston fired the Stern torpedo which missed and after about an hour the guns crew scored a direct hit on the merchant ship at which stage the sub-chaser withdrew to aid the damaged ship.
During a lull in the fighting a bucket-chain was established to bail out water using the officers and crews 'heads'*, Able seaman Wild produced about 20 buckets which he had 'won' prior to sailing.
As the diving compass on the bridge had been hit and the Gyro compass was flooded, we were being guided by 'faithful freddy' (a boat compass) which TGM Tommy Gates supported on his knees. At approximately 0900 Wt. Eng. Hodge reported the Port engine had seized and there was little hope of it functioning again, at the same time 'Guts' Harmer fell overboard and as the water had not yet reached the main motors Swanston stopped, manoeuvred and recovered him. He continued to 'gripe' over the loss of his much prized boots. Course was resumed on one engine at a speed of 7 knots. I then joined 'Guts' and we added extra strength to the bucket chain. Later 'Guts' then went onto the bridge and acted as an air lookout until dark, taking occasional bursts with a Tommy gun on very close aircraft.**

*Lavatory

**During this patrol Shakespeare suffered some 75 separate air attacks.

The Holes!

Note loss of W/T Insulator covering plate 'Top right'

At 0930 a seaplane sighted over Nankauri Strait, started a low level dive bombing attack from astern. When the range had closed sufficiently, a short burst from the starboard Vicker's gun manned by P.O. Ted Jones (2nd Coxswain) caused him to release a bomb 20 yards away on the port side, and was seen to crash into the sea about 1000 yards off the starboard bow. At 1000 two 'Jakes' appeared and carried out a diving low-level attack and then came in and bombed us. The splash from one bomb flooded the bridge and burst a HP airline in the bilges. There was a general feeling that we had been holed again and might have to abandon ship! Up to 1420, five more attacks by Jakes each carrying 50lb bombs were made and further subsequent attacks were diverted by Vicker's gun and Oerlikon fire.

At 1420 an unidentified vessel was seen closing from the starboard quarter. On sighting this, all deciphered signals and patrol orders were burned under the guidance and authority of Sub Lt. William Grey RNVR. The code books and silhouette photos were sacked ready for ditching, and the two torpedoes were brought to the ready. A bomber and two fighter bombers now appeared and one fighter carrying two bombs made a dive attack at an angle of 75 degrees, dropped his bombs and made a machine gun attack. The bomber came in at a height of about 3000 ft and had a near miss with two heavy (1000lb) bombs on the port side, seriously wounding Able Seaman T. A. Motterham who died the following day. Able Seaman G. Taylor also died from injuries sustained while in the bucket-chain.

From 1600 until just before sunset single attacks by groups of four aircraft, fighter bombers with machine guns, occurred at half hourly intervals. The Oerlikon finally jammed and could not be cleared. The 3" gun was used throughout the day. Some 200 rounds were fired, using all time fused shell, and then when these were expended changes were made to fuse other shells. At 1830 just before sunset, a bomber, two fighter bombers and a seaplane carried out attacks from the sun and were circling in and out of the clouds but no further damage was done. With darkness the air attacks ceased and it was possible to take stock of the situation below which was as follows:

1. Port engine out of action. Starboard engine in fair shape.
2. Auxiliary oil and water pumps out of action due to flooding.
3. main motors out of action due to flooding.

4. W/T and giro compass out of action by flooding.
5. Ship being steered by Evershed from control room, using ships tele motor aft.
6. Hole 10" by 5" in pressure hull.
7. Hole in gun tower.
8. Diving compass out of action.
9. Hole in no.2 port main ballast tank.
10. 4" depth of water in control room. Battery boards tight.
11. Starboard side high pressure ring-main severed outside W/T office.
12. Low pressure blower line slightly damaged.
13. Battery apparently undamaged and in use through emergency circuits. (Density 1202.)
14. Ballast pump out of action.
15. Upper conning tower hatch could not be shut.

Casualties numbered 15, two later died.

Ken said to me: "This is the only ad hoc committee I attended during my service career." (KTN-B)

The ships company was then organised for the night, a chain of buckets still being necessary to deal with water entering through the damaged pressure hull.
On the morning of the 4th January the port circulator was rigged as a bilge pump, and a suction obtained in the control room. A hammock was rigged as a chute, so that the water from the hull ran into the engine room bilges. Work was started on the seized cylinder (no.7) port engine, but the spare cylinder and piston stowed in the after end of the motor room were under water and work was therefore abandoned.
At dawn the Vicker's guns were stripped and cleaned, and an attempt was made to get the Oerlikon to work in readiness to repel another days air attack. A heavy rainstorm obscured the eastern horizon for more than two hours after dawn. To our great relief and surprise nothing occurred throughout the day, *many agnostics were converted.* Ted Jones (2nd Cox.) then went over the side and with soap and Hedley's compound improved the blanket plugging which considerably reduced the input of water. I then reminded Lt. Lutley that a signal stating that HMS/M Stygian was outward bound for patrol had been received the

Taken During The Action

Canoe from HMS/M Stygian at daylight after we contacted her in the darkness, just!! Bringing urgent medical supplies. Ken Wade left on bandstand.

previous night, this was recovered from the W/T office and deciphered again. Course was set to place Shakespeare on Stygian's route.
On the 5th January at 0900 it was decided to put an external patch on the hull to make it more sea worthy, using rubber insertion, soap, part of the steel bridge chart table, two McMahon spanners as strongbacks and clips and bolts from the reload torpedo safety bands. The repair was finished at 1400. This enabled speed to be increased to 8fi knots. A spare semi-rotary pump was also rigged to remove water from the engine room bilges.
At 2100 it was decided to fire recognition grenades at each hour and very-lights of the same colour every half hour (to conserve grenades) and to fire a star shell every two hours through the night or until HMS/M Stygian challenged. The White Ensign was then laid on the fore casing, a risk if spotted by any enemy aircraft but considered an aid to or survival.
On the 6th January at 0100 a light was sighted to westward and shortly after we exchanged pendants with Stygian. We burnt navigation lights as we were manoeuvring with difficulty. Stygian suspecting a trap, in spite of correct recognition grenade, asked for the Christian name of our commanding officers wife, as both commanding officers were personal friends. We replied the name of our commanding officers wife is Sheila and that your wife's name is Stella. Details of damage, casualties etc. was passed for transmission.
At 0200 in company with Stygian course was set for Trincomalee. At 0900 both submarines stopped and Stygian sent over a working party of six ratings, torches, medical supplies aboard, by a Folboat, and informed us that HMS Raider would be meeting us about 1530. On arrival all 16 wounded and injured were transferred to her and Stygian proceeded for patrol.
On 7th January at 1000, water was now so low in the engine room and motor room bilges that the starboard shaft which had been cooled by it now fired up at the bulkhead gland, and the starboard engine practically stopped; then it was found the shaft had dropped. A tow was passed after some difficulty to HMS Raider. At 1030 towing commenced the speed working up to 15 knots in an endeavour to get in before nightfall. At 1200 the tow parted at our end owing to a break in one of the studless links adjacent to the joining shackle. At 1205 after repassing a 4fi" wire during which operation Raider's stern swung onto our bow, and caused a neat cut in her side. At 1300 Raider was relieved by HMS

Whelp. The 1st Lt. of HMS Whelp was H.R.H. Prince Phillip (now the Duke of Edinburgh). I recall Lt. Lutley informing me that the officer supervising the tow was a royal prince. My reply at that stage did less than justice to the monarchy which I admire and respect. At 1800 the resumed tow at Whelp's end parted and with great difficulty we hauled this in sufficiently to unshackle our end of the 4fi" wire, this was then secured to a rope from the destroyer and after necessary adjustments was again passed to us and shackled on. During this operation Whelp was also holed!
On the 8th January at 0500 we passed Foul Point and assisted by a tug secured alongside HMS Wolfe.
My first sight was 'Guts' Harmer immaculately dressed leaning on the guard rail, a rare and special experience.*

Decorations awarded for this action

DSO Lt. David Swanston DSC★
DSC Lt. Lutley, Sub Lt. Morgan
CGM P.O.Tel Harmer
DSM P.O. Jones, L. Tel. Wade, CERA McAlistair, E.R.A Coker,
L. Sto. Hollis, Sto. Wray, A.B. Gibbons

Six mention in despatches were also awarded.

In narrating this action after nearly 50 years, I place on record the encouragement I have recieved from Keith Nethercoate-Bryant, Chairman Gatwick SOCA. Also the help of Ken Curry and Frank Gapper, who were the youngest members of the crew and have enabled me to fill in the details which with the passage of time needed confirmation.
Last but not least this story would not have been possible without the help of my dear wife Betty, who has acted as my scribe. Little did she realise that obtaining a photo of the Shakespeare would lead to the losing one room of our home to the countless books and photographs of submarine memorabilia.

Dr. Ken Wade DSM.

* Harmer had been taken onto Raider as one of the wounded - he had burnt feet (KTN-B).

ERA Coker hauled aboard after inspecting damage during action.

HMS Whelp taking off dead and dying and bringing working party to stop the b... water coming aboard. H.R.H. Prince Phillip was 1st Lt. of H.M.S. Whelp.

Alongside 'Wolfe'

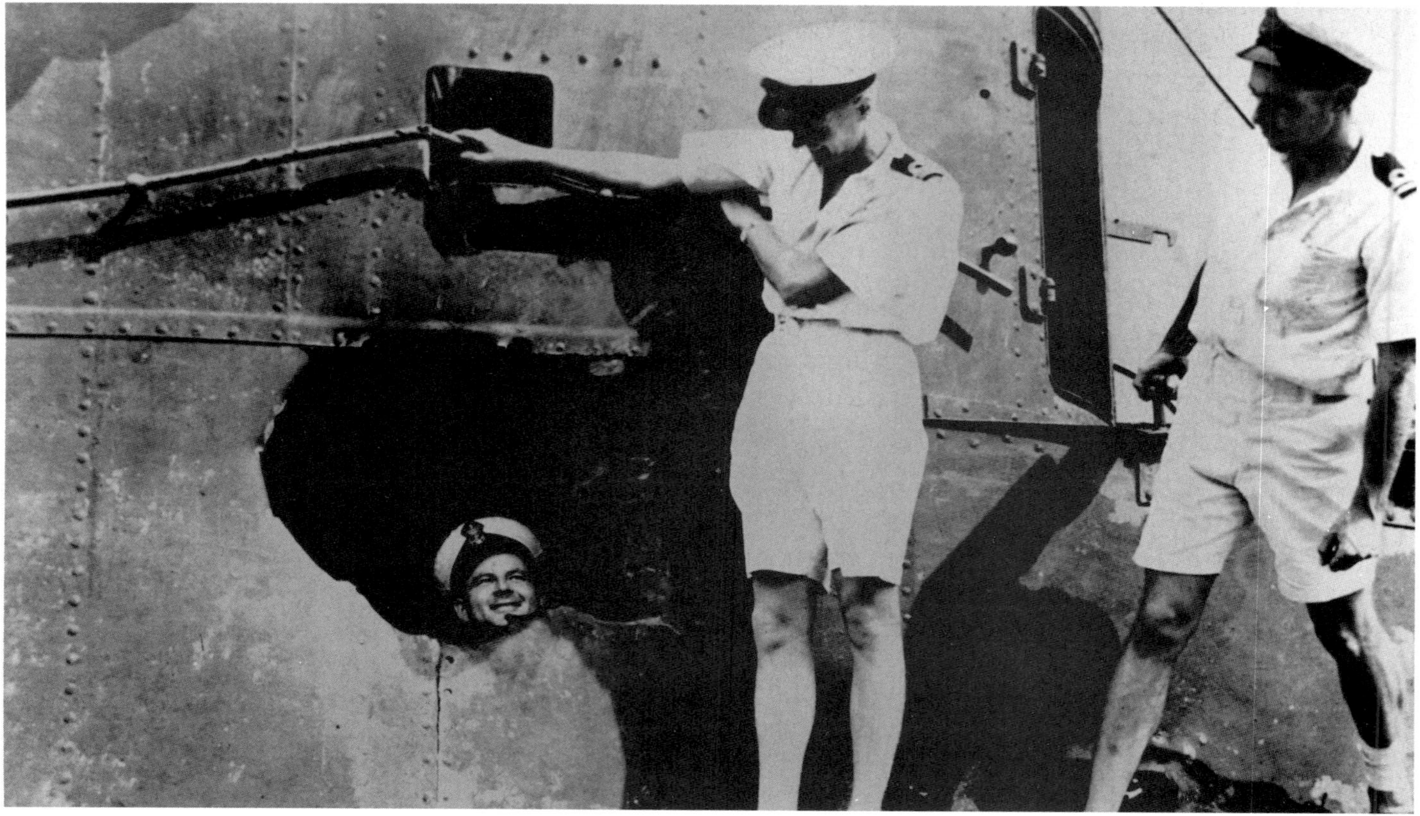

(L to R) P.O. George Harmer CGM, Lt. David Swanston DSO, DSC★, Lt. John Lutley DSC.

Inspecting the damage alongside 'Wolfe'

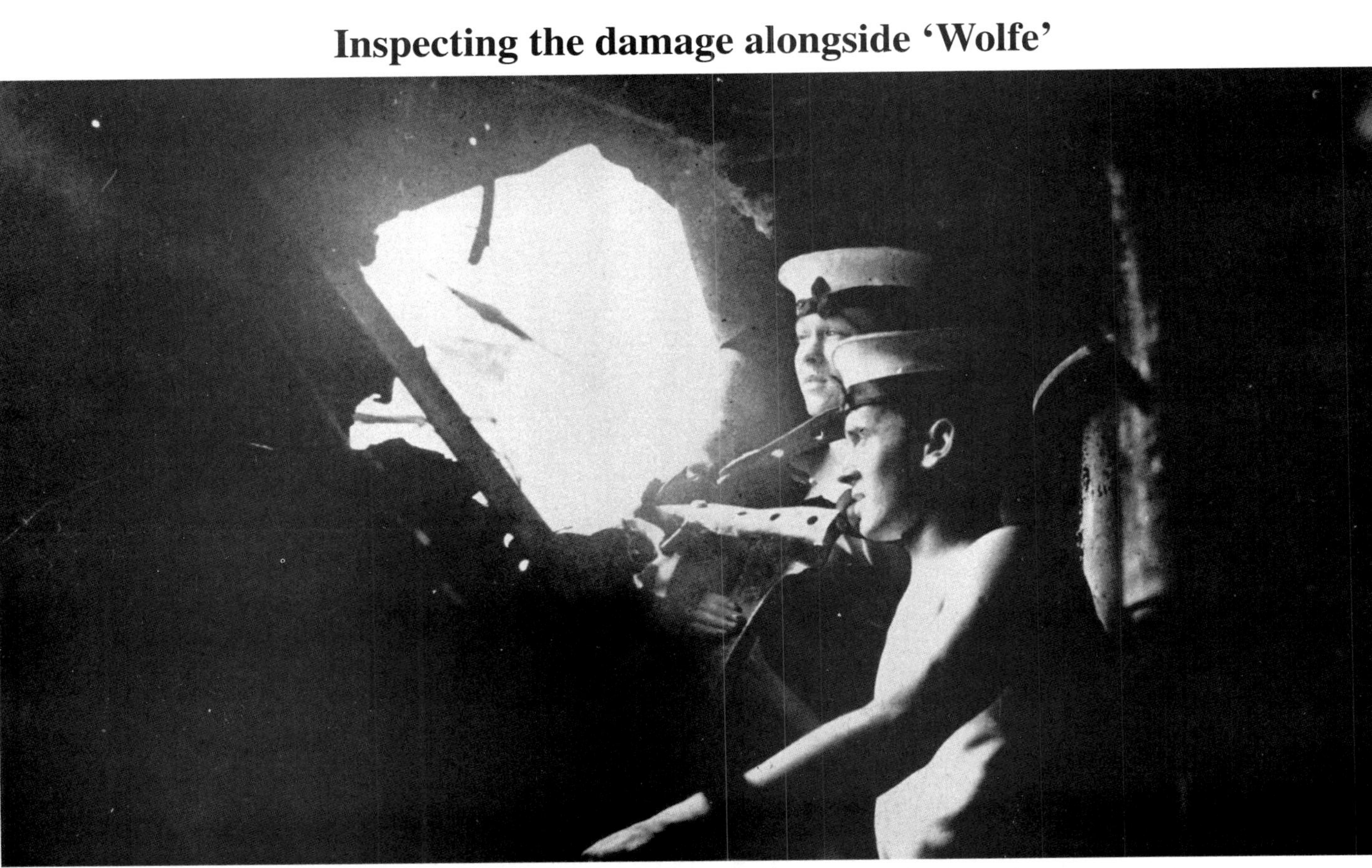

The hole in the pressure hull was outside w/t office adjacent to bulkhead door to engine room.

Back in Ceylon Alongside Wolfe

The Survivors!